IRENE W. HUSTON

THAT
DOOR

A Memoir
Dedicated to Ending
Generational Sexual Abuse

Foreword by Dr. Beverly "BAM" Crawford

THAT
DOOR

TO THE READER

This story is true and based on my life. It happened in the South in the state of Mississippi during the 1940's. Pseudo names replace true characters to protect individuals who are represented throughout the book.

DEDICATION

I dedicate this book to my late husband, Ralph Huston, and to my mom, Dovie Wade, who helped form the spirit of Christ within me throughout the years. To them, I am truly grateful. To my children, thank you for always being there, for believing in me, and for selflessly sharing me with the world. I love you all so much.

TABLE OF CONTENTS

ACKNOWLEDGEMENTS

I would like to say that the book you are holding in your hands would not be without the endless focus and care of my spiritual daughter Shanene Higgins. Prayer was made over every chapter that people would be touched and healed through the inspired written words throughout this book. I would like to personally thank her for never giving up on me in completing this assignment. She knew it was not about her. Thank God for sending her into my life. She has truly been a blessing.

My thanks and appreciation to my editor, Chris Kelly, whom I have only known for a short time. She saw a need and worked diligently in taking this project and bringing it to its fruition. I further want to acknowledge her care, her love, and her dedication in providing my story's enhanced content. Thank you so much.

Many thanks to my best friend and colleague, Pastor Donja Carr, an anchor of stability who ran side-by-side with me through so much. She pushed me and was a constant source of encouragement to me for many years in the ministry. Whenever the Lord would speak to me about a project or a given direction for the ministry, she would listen and wait until she heard me say, "The Lord said..." and then would immediately say, "As long as the Lord said to do it, I am with you." Rest in peace dear friend.

Thanks and appreciation also to Cynthia McKelvy who has faithfully stood with the ministry for over 30 years and is yet standing. Thank you for your years of dedicated service.

To the entire Global Christian Ministries family and to every supportive person who has ever prayed, encouraged, and pushed the work of God forward, I appreciate you. May God continue to increase you on every side. I could not have made it without your love and support.

Finally, I would like to reach back to my childhood and thank the YWCA for investing in my life when I volunteered to help hand out clothing to the needy during the summertime, which gave me the opportunity to go to summer camp for free. Upon my arrival at the campground, I discovered we would be sleeping out in the open on cots. I began to cry and wrote my parents to come pick me up. But then one day while I was walking in the woods I discovered a big treehouse. I immediately thought about what an adventure it would be to sleep in that treehouse. After inquiring about it, I learned that I would have to come back to camp for two more years before I could earn the right to sleep there. Despite being fearful of sleeping outside, my desire for the adventure was stronger than the fear. (We are stronger than we think we are)! I pushed through the yearly camping challenges and my fears because I had a goal. (Always have a goal and stay focused on it)! After sleeping outdoors on cots the first year, we got to sleep in covered wagons the second year. Finally, the third year came with all the anticipation of sleeping in the big treehouse; but that year I had a frightening experience. I almost drowned but never yelled out for help. I was conditioned to keep quiet amidst fear and danger. As I was sinking down into the water, I remembered my swimming instructor telling me that if I dog-paddled I would not drown; so I put the word she spoke into action and made it to shore safely. Faith comes by hearing and acting on the Word of God. Putting the spoken word into action saved my life. Because of the YWCA experiences, I no longer had the fear of swimming or sleeping outside. I lost fear amidst fear itself. Facing my fears changed my life and unknowingly prepared me to face challenges that would come later in life. I now know that God had specially equipped me with a drive to achieve beyond obstacles that appear to be real. When I returned to school after that camp, I immediately went to the diving board and jumped off. The swimming instructor wanted to know what happened to make me so bold. I never told her; but I knew on the inside what God had done. Always remember that no matter what trials you go through, the plan of God will prevail and come full circle in your life. The scary things are the very things that will catapult you into your destiny if you can let go of the rope and allow yourself to fall into the arms of your heavenly Father. He will never drop you. He will never hurt you.

TESTIMONIALS

Irene, I am so blessed to have you as a sister and friend. Keep on soaring and treading upon unplowed territory. You are truly gifted by God. I love you sis!-- *Ollie Jean*

I know this book will be life-changing for all who read it. You have been an inspiration to me as well as others with your ministry/ministerial gift, and your desire for others to fulfill their God-given purpose. Love you and God Bless!-- *Alberta Huston*

I met Dr. Huston several years ago. When we first met, she was a wife, a momma, great housekeeper, and homemaker. She and her husband worked fervently in church activities and raised their children in the church. At the time I first met her, we both attended Olive Grove Baptist Church in Berkeley, California. When her husband began Global Christian Ministry, Dr. Huston was his faithful support system. She worked in the background while he received all the accolades. She has since become a pastor, an author, and an international speaker. I moved to New York, but we kept in communication. One day, while visiting a mutual friend of ours, she confided to me that, "The Lord keeps telling me about having a women's faith seminar." The next year, Dr. Huston, Pastor Donja Carr, and I held the first initial Women's Faith Seminar. Until Dr. Huston began to hold Irene's Women's Faith Foundation seminars and conferences, I had never heard of any women's conferences. She is a pioneer in this field. I really don't believe that Dr. Huston has any idea of the comprehensive network she has seeded in ministry. She has brought people together who would never have met. I really don't think she realizes how important her function has been in so many women's lives, or how it has affected blessings on others whom she probably will never meet until we are all called home to glory. I am thankful that I have been able to share with the reader some of the outstanding attributes of Dr. Irene MOMMA Huston.-- *Ernestine Sanders, PhD*

Dr. Apostle Irene Huston and her message are timeless. Her story is fresh for the present generation of men and women who feel trapped in abuse and hopeless to get out. The story is written with such deep conviction, transparency, and humility that it is hard to put down. God's healing, deliverance, and hope for thousands of desperate individuals are laced throughout the pages of this book. This work is a definite answer for a host of problems plaguing our society today.-- *Chris Kelly*

THAT DOOR is a mind transforming experience penned to bring a victim from behind dark doors of bondage to bright doors of freedom through the light of God. His transforming light obliterates every door of darkness and ushers the victim to a door of total victory. THAT DOOR is graphic but presents an easy-to-read and hard to put down piece of work. The clarity and flow of its presentation invites and commands the reader to look resolutely to its conclusion. Carmen's experiences were dark and dismal, and were it not for God, hers could have been a life lost and wasted forever. Instead, her painful journey through dark doors allowed her to stand as one touched by the feelings and infirmities of many, and her doors of victory have shed light on the way forward for many. This work vividly illustrates that in spite of being locked behind doors of darkness, submission to the true and Living God can transfer any individual to doors which secure purpose and destiny. The door governing the plans of God for every life can be experienced as indicated by the promises of Almighty God in Jeremiah 29:11.—*Apostle Magdalena Griffith, Barbados, West Indies*

FOREWORD BY
DR. BEVERLY 'BAM' CRAWFORD

Dr. Irene W. Huston has been a friend and colleague of mine for many years, and I don't know anyone more qualified to deal with the sensitive issue of child sexual abuse that plagues our society. I wish this book had been written many years ago, as it tells the story for many of "us" who were molested as children. It gives us a voice and others a glimpse into the pain of violated children.

Abuse is any behavior that is designed to control and subjugate another human being through the use of fear or verbal and physical assaults, to make that person feel devalued. These things cut to the very core of the abused. Core feelings that are borne in an environment of abuse strangle emotional and developmental growth. However, if you or someone you know has been abused, it is possible to learn to overcome that abuse and become productive, valuable citizens of society. Change is possible for you or anyone you know who has been abused if you are willing to work hard, persevere, and understand the benefits of revival in your thinking. The power of the soul can guide you into wholeness, restoration, renewal, and healing in the rebuilding of your hopes and dreams.

Since God has not given us a spirit of fear; it is vitally important that we utilize His gifts of power, love, and intelligence to renew our minds. Dr. Huston's personal journey from molestation to recovery offers hope and help for the "damaged soul." Life is full of change and redefinition. *That*

Door is a heart-wrenching story; a story that challenges a renewal of the mind and encourages the pursuit of a journey to restore the damaged soul. — *Beverly "Bam" Crawford, D.D.*, Author and Senior Pastor

INTRODUCTION

Carmen was constantly reminded that all adults were safe, but what she experienced from someone who was supposed to love and protect her caused uncertainty within her and made her become unstable in her thinking. The instability of her mind made her doubt everything about herself. She shut down emotionally and learned to suppress what she should have been able to verbally express to a responsible adult.

When her uncle began molesting her, he instilled the spirit of fear within her. He told her not to tell anyone or he would hurt her even more. Carmen obeyed her uncle as she had been taught to do. She became confused because her uncle told her she was special, but she wasn't supposed to tell anyone why she was so special. At the tender age of seven, Carmen was already perplexed about what true love is and who she was. When she felt something just did not feel right in her mind, she kept it to herself. She was confused on many levels because of the lack of communication in her family about forbidden topics. Sex was a topic that was never discussed.

Carmen was very well taken care of financially, but her emotions were in turmoil. There was nothing she was in need of materially. What Carmen really needed was the emotional support of those who said they loved her. She did not get that support. She was afraid to speak out because, in her family, it was a sign of disrespect for a child to speak because the adults were always right. Carmen was required to do what she was told to do. Therefore, she learned to suppress her feelings, even when she was hurting. Because of fear, she submitted to her uncle when he overpowered and molested her. She developed a tendency in her posture to turn her head to the side because of the abuse. Carmen was forced into a position of unnatural submission, and therefore started to believe that she had no way out of the situation, that what happened to her was just a part of life. The only time she felt somewhat useful was when trying to please her parents by making sure she did everything they asked to the best of her ability. She felt she wasn't allowed to make any mistakes. When she did make a mistake, she was afraid to explain what had happened. To make matters worse, she didn't have the luxury of being a child. Being the oldest daughter, she had many chores, including learning to cook at the age of nine.

The abuse Carmen suffered from her uncle caused a disconnection to take place within her. She became paralyzed in her thinking and could no longer feel. Because she was continually molested, her outward demeanor began to change. She became withdrawn and illusive. She no longer talked unless she was forced to. She became a recluse, and no one acknowledged the difference in her behavior--not even her parents. Carmen tried to tell them the best way she knew how, but they ignored the signs that she was being sexually abused. Her parents loved her and tried to give her everything she needed. Like most little girls, she was especially close to her dad.

Carmen's parents would leave her in the care of her brother who was also young and unstable. She was, therefore, in essence alone with no one to talk to who would acknowledge her cry for help. She was a child who had to try and figure things out on her own. Being unable to share her problem with someone led her into a viscous cycle of blaming herself for the abuse she suffered. Her voice was heard but ignored. Her tears were seen but wiped away as if they didn't exist. She was a child who had to fight long and hard for her sanity. Internally, Carmen was and is a determined fighter, but outwardly she was paralyzed by her cruel circumstances. As a victim of incest, she never sought help. She made a vow of silence to herself, and therefore kept the suffering of incest within her until she was thirty-five years old.

CARMEN SPEAKS

I, Dr. Irene W. Huston, decided at the age of thirty-five that I would open my mouth and heart, and speak about the travesties that occurred in my life. When I made the choice to forgive my uncle and free myself through speaking out in women's meetings about what happened to me, inner-healing release began. I felt a heavy load had been lifted from off my back. However, I still craved the acceptance of others and strove to be perfect in everything I did. God is still working on me, but I am now complete in Him as I share my childhood experiences to touch and bring deliverance to suffering individuals with hope and answers. I am willing to be transparent as I pour out my beliefs from my heart.

I hope that my experiences will expose patterns for others to recognize and know that the ideals of women and men can be corrupt. I am not a psychologist. I am speaking from experiences. My late husband and I counseled couples together. We both shared our journey, our mistakes, and consequences in dealing with our choices. My husband made a point to communicate how much he valued and loved me, even amid trying times. It is my prayer for the readers of this book to know and understand that you do not have to bear the burden of shame alone. Shame is just a trick of Satan to make you miss your purpose in life. Realize that what happened to you was not your fault. Give your cares to Jesus Christ. He will heal you from the pains of your past. You too can live again and finally be truly free. ~~*Dr. Irene W. Huston*

Irene, Age 7

Chapter One

I'M A BIG GIRL NOW

I still vividly recall the beautiful sunny day as I played in my grandparent's home in Mississippi. My little sister and I were running to get on the swing. Just as I was running toward the swing, I heard my uncle call my name.

"Carmen, come here for a minute. Come quickly, Carmen!"

I hurriedly ran in the direction of his voice, excited to see why he was calling me. Could it be that he brought me a brand new toy from the store? Or maybe it was something else that I told him I wanted. I ran all the way from the yard to the house with all the energy of a seven-year-old child. I approached the porch steps as he swung open the screen door.

"Come inside. I have a surprise for you."

I jumped up and down with excitement. I was so happy.

"That's what I like to see," he laughed.

I followed him inside. I walked through the front door as he looked at me and smiled.

"What is it, Uncle?"

"Just you wait and see. I have something that's going to make you very happy. Let's go in the kitchen."

"Okay!"

We went into my grandparent's kitchen. He opened the refrigerator door and took out a tub of vanilla ice cream. I ate so much ice cream and laughed so hard that my stomach hurt.

"I love vanilla ice cream. It's my favorite!" I said gleefully.

"I know, but this is just the beginning of your surprise."

I was so full that I was bursting with joy and excitement, because my uncle had been so nice to me.

"I have another surprise for you," he said. "Come with me into the living room. Now close your eyes, Carmen."

I shut my eyes tightly. Then I heard him open a door.

"Don't peek now. Don't peek."

"I promise, Uncle. I promise I won't peek."

"Okay, now you can open your eyes."

I opened my eyes. He was holding a big bag. It was the biggest bag I had ever seen. I remember my momma telling me that her uncle gave it to her when she was my age.

"I love it! I love it! What's inside?"

"Open it up and see."

I grabbed and opened with all the tenacity and strength of a seven-year-old child because I couldn't wait to see what was in the bag. It had to be something special because the bag was so big. I couldn't believe my eyes when I opened it.

"Thank you, Uncle! Thank you for the pretty dress with ruffles in the front and buttons down the back!"

I took the dress and rubbed it gently along my cheek. It felt soft. "Oh my gosh! It's just as soft as my pillow."

"Which pillow?" he asked.

"My pretty pink pillow. The one that's big and fluffy. The pillow that Momma bought me for Christmas so I wouldn't be afraid to sleep in my bed."

"Oh...that pillow. I'm glad you like it as much as your bedtime pillow. Are you ready for your next surprise?"

"I have another surprise?" I asked with even greater excitement.

"Yes, you do. But before I show you the next surprise, you have to put this new dress on."

"Okay, Uncle."

I jumped up and started to take my play clothes off.

"No, not here. You have to change your clothes in there."

I ran to the other room and changed into my new dress. My uncle called me his special niece, and I felt special. Then I heard him call me.

"Carmen, are you ready for your next surprise?"

I darted out the door and ran back into the front room, but he wasn't there. I heard him call me again.

"Carmen, where are you?"

"I'm coming, Uncle!"

I ran toward his voice from one room to the next. The closer I got the more excited I became. Then I ran into his room, and there he was, standing by his closet door next to a dresser that my momma told me had been in the family for years. I started to laugh because I didn't think he was very good at playing hide and seek.

"Ha! Ha! I found you! I found you! You can't hide from me."

"Yes, you got me. You found me! You're good at following my voice. How do you like your new pretty dress?"

"I love it! I love it so much that I never want to take it off. I look pretty, don't I, Uncle? Don't I look pretty?"

"You sure do, and my special niece should have what she likes."

He opened the top dresser drawer and pulled out a big red apple.

"Uncle, is that another surprise?"

"Yes, it's just for you."

He opened the bag and gave the apple to me. It was so big that I had to hold it with both hands. I was so excited that I ran around the room and started jumping up and down. I was so happy. Then he picked me up and kissed me on the cheek.

"I love you, Carmen. You are so special to me." Then he put me on his bed. I was still laughing with excitement. I began to roll around on the bed until I ran out of breath.

"Whooo! I can hardly breathe."

My uncle laughed, sat down beside me, and began to stroke my hair. I laid there on my back and sighed loudly because I was so happy with all the surprises. My uncle is the best uncle ever, I thought to myself.

"I'm glad that you like all the surprises," he said. He told me to lie on my stomach and unbuttoned my dress. He slid my dress off and I got cold and started sneezing.

"I'm cold, Uncle."

"Stop whining. Keep still and be quiet!"

His voice changed, and I started to feel strange. He was touching me in my private place with his fingers. I started to squirm because it hurt, and then I began to cry.

"Stay still and stop crying," he growled. "I told you to stay still. The pain is good for you!"

It was hard for me not to make any noise because he was hurting me. But I was always taught to obey adults, so I squeezed my eyes shut, pressed my lips together, and softly cried. He made all sorts of funny noises as he kept touching me and said my name repeatedly.

"Oh yeah, that's what I want," he said, breathing heavily and out of control. "There, right there, Carmen. Now, give me your hand."

Out of fear, I obeyed and gave him my hand. He rested his hand on mine and made strange movements and sounds as our hands moved up and down faster and faster. Then I felt something wet on my hand. I was so confused and very afraid. I felt sick to my stomach; yet I remained silent, afraid of what he would do if I uttered a sound. Then his body shook and jerked. I didn't know what was happening, so I pinched my eyes together tighter and tighter as he moaned and yelled out loudly. As he continued to force my hand, he cried, and I cringed, unable to fathom what he would do next. But then, he fell asleep. I silently cried as I watched him toss and turn until he was facing me with an evil grin, daring me not to move nor speak.

"Okay, Carmen, it's time for you to go back outside and play on the swing. Remember, you'll always be special to me."

He picked me up off the bed, set me down on the floor and gave me my clothes. He grabbed both my ears with his big, strong hands and looked right into my eyes and whispered, "Now don't tell anyone about this, because you're a big girl now." I nodded my head in agreement and walked slowly out of the room because I was afraid to run. I went into the other room and put my play clothes back on. I went back outside but I didn't want to swing anymore. My older brother, Gary, was pushing my little sister, Trease. She was laughing hard and having fun.

Then my brother started asking me questions without giving me a chance to answer. "Why did you go inside? What were you doing? Why are you looking sad?"

The screen door swung open, and my uncle started walking off the porch toward me, fixing his pants and pulling on his suspenders. I told Trease it was my turn because I didn't want to go back inside. She jumped off and started playing with her doll. My uncle got closer, cleared his throat, and spit out some snuff. He put his hands on the swing, shook the ropes, and whispered in my ear.

"Why you ain't swangin', gal? Don't just sit there like a bump on a log. Hush that crying!"

I wanted to cry even more, but I couldn't. I just wanted him to go away, but he started to push me back and forth on the swing and kept yanking the ropes. I wished he would stop; but instead, he kept pushing me even more and asked me questions that I didn't want to answer.

"How did you like your surprises? Do you think, Trease would like a surprise too?

"What surprise?" asked Trease.

"Surprises are for big girls only," I told her.

"I'm a big girl. I'm a big girl, too!" she insisted.

"No you're not, and you never will be!" She started to cry.

"Stop whining like a baby," my brother told her.

"Carmen, you didn't answer me. How did you like your surprises?" my uncle asked again. "You liked 'em didn't you?"

At first, I didn't say anything, but I was afraid of what he might do to my sister, so I hesitantly said yes.

"That's what I thought. You and me have something special. Ain't that right, Carmen? Cause you know your uncle loves you, don't ya?"

"Yes, Uncle."

Then he looked at Gary and said, "All girls like surprises. All girls do. Big ones, little ones. It don't matter. Remember that, son. Give a gift, get a treat."

"What kind of treat?" Gary asked.

"Come on in the house, so I can school you boy!" They started back to the house. As they walked to the porch, my uncle looked over his shoulder and blew a kiss at me. I was glad that he didn't take my little sister back inside the house with him. I just needed to protect Trease as long as I could, or at least until my grandma came back from the store.

I stayed outside the rest of the day with Trease while she played on the swing, until it started to get dark and our grandma called us inside.

"Carmen and Trease, come on in the house now. It's getting late."

My little sister ran in front of me into my grandma's arms.

"Baby, baby, you are such a cutie pie. Grandma just loves to kiss your Treasy cheeks."

I walked slowly to the house because I knew my uncle was inside. I walked as slowly as my feet could carry me until my grandma told me to speed it up.

"Carmen, why are you moving so slowly? You have to go to school in the morning. Come on now!"

I stopped at the porch.

"Come on in here. It's getting late, and you need to take a bath."

I stepped onto the porch and went inside. My uncle was sitting on the couch, the same couch where he gave me the big bag of treats! He looked at me and smiled, "Did you have fun on the swing?"

I just kept walking, as if I didn't hear him, right past my grandma.

"Carmen, didn't you hear your uncle talking to you? You were raised better than that."

"Yes, Grandma, I heard him."

"Then turn around and answer him."

"Yes, Uncle, I had fun."

"That's good, Carmen. So did I."

I walked slowly away from him to go take my bath. My grandma had prepared my bath water for me in the tub.

"Now Carmen, get undressed while I go and get your pajamas."

When she came back, I still had my play clothes on. "Awww Carmen, you are as slow as ice cream rising! Come on now. Be a good little girl and take your bath."

I locked the bathroom door because I was afraid my uncle would come in. After my bath and I was all dressed, I slowly opened the door and looked out to see where my uncle was. I didn't see him, but I saw my grandma in the kitchen. I moved swiftly towards my grandma, told her I was done with my bath, and kissed her good night.

"Don't you want me to tuck you in and give you a good night kiss like I usually do?"

"That's okay Grandma. I'm a big girl now. I want to give *you* a kiss."

"Okay baby."

She smiled as I gave her a big kiss.

"I'll see you in the morning baby."

I went to the room and sat on the floor because I was afraid to get in the bed. I just stared at the bed as my body shook and shivered. Then I heard my uncle's voice pounding in my head. *"Don't tell anyone. Stop whining like a little girl. Keep still and be quiet. Remember, you're a big girl now."* The door opened and I heard a squeaking sound. I closed my eyes, leaned over, and buried my face in my lap. I made sure I didn't say a word.

TRUST

When Carmen was a child there was a tradition in her household and possibly in a large percentage of American households of not discussing how young girls' bodies grow and develop. Carmen was too young to differentiate her love for God and what she thought were the obligations of being 'special'. Her young mind was wondering why special nieces got such lovely dresses and jewelry. In Carmen's generation, young girls saw very few images of women working outside of the home and being able to purchase beautiful dresses or jewelry for themselves. Of course a lovely dress would enhance a young girl's self-esteem.

Families who have a man in the house with emotional or mental problems should make every effort to seek adult day care for the individual and family counseling for everyone else in the home.

The secret code of silence about development of the body, sex, and adult behavior compounded Carmen's problem and prevented her from knowing how to protect herself when being inappropriately approached by the opposite sex. The secret code of silence made her too afraid to expose her uncle's behavior. Teaching very young children what is appropriate and inappropriate touching is critical in this generation where child pornography and sex trafficking has become rampant. Teaching them who and who not to trust based on the identification of wrong behaviors will certainly reduce their fear of telling when something is not right. Proper teaching will give them the courage to run from wrong behaviors lessen the occurrences of child abductions which have risen to an all-time high in recent years.

Carmen was just a child, but because of what happened to her, she was forced to grow up much too fast. She had been touched in an inappropriate way by someone who said he loved her and whom she was supposed to be able to trust, which left her confused. Because she was just a child, she confused the love of God with the lust of man. This greatly damaged her self-esteem. It left her in a state of uncertainty as to who she was, both as a person and as a child of God. Both her mind and body had been violated which caused her to form inappropriate ideas about what love was and what it was not.

Maybe someone has violated you in the same way, and you have found yourself in a pattern of not knowing who to trust. Maybe at the moment you thought you could trust someone, they deceived you, and you fell back into the same damaging state-of-mind. You may have even told yourself you would never trust anyone again. If this is you, God, your ever-loving and never-changing Father, wants you to know that you can trust Him--completely. He will never hurt you. He will never violate the beautiful masterpiece He has created called *you.* I know trusting is not always easy, but you can begin to trust God one step at a time.

Lean on, trust in, and be confident in the Lord with all your heart and mind and do not rely on your own insight or understanding. In all your ways know, recognize, and acknowledge Him, and He will direct and make straight and plain your paths. Proverbs 3:5-6 - (AMP)

Chapter Two

HE TOUCHED MY HEART WITH LAUGHTER

"Hey baby, why are you sitting on the floor?" my grandma asked. I popped my head up.

"Grandma, I'm too scared to get in the bed."

"Little Angel, why on earth are you afraid to get in the bed? I made it all comfy for you and your sister. I also put your pretty pink pillow and two warm blankets on the bed. I knew my grandbabies would be spending the night tonight, so I wanted to make sure that my little angels would be well taken care of. I even put something special for y'all under the covers. Then I sprinkled the covers with Grandma's love and kisses. Are you sure you don't want to get in the bed?"

"I . . . I'm not sure."

"Baby, God doesn't give us a spirit of fear. He gives us a spirit of power, love, and a sound mind. You don't have nothing to be afraid of, and Grandma's right here. So come over here and let me tuck you in."

I slowly got up and walked toward her. She picked me up and gently laid me on the bed.

"There you go, Little Angel."

"Thank you, Grandma."

"No problem, sweetie. Your grandma loves you. I'd do just about anything for you. Don't you know that by now?"

"You would do anything?"

"Just about, baby. What's on your mind?"

"Grandma, do you think that I am a big girl?"

"I sure do."

"Then why are you tucking me in?"

"Big girls get tucked in too, and they should always be treated with love and care. That's why I want to tuck you in. I want you to know that I love you so very much. You are very special to me, and I want you to grow up to be all that God created you to be. I know that you are getting to be a big girl now; but no matter how big you get, remember that you'll always be loved and cherished--especially by me and your grandpa. Now go to sleep. It's past your bedtime."

"Grandma, can I ask you one more thing?"

"Sure baby, just one more. It's getting late."

"How did you know that Grandpa loved you?"

"Well, Little Angel, I knew your grandpa loved me because of the way he prayed, and he made sure he always gave me his very best--no half-stepping with him. He would always make sure that I had nice things because he wanted to make me happy. He was a funny one, your grandpa. He could always make me laugh, even when times weren't so good."

"You weren't always happy, Grandma?"

"No baby, not always. When your uncle was drafted to fight for our country, we got worried that he wouldn't make it home from the war. But we trusted God and prayed every day for his safety, regardless of what we heard on the radio. We prayed and prayed, and God brought him home. Some people said that he was better off there because of what the war did to his mind."

"What happened to his mind?"

"Every time he hears a car engine, it's like he's right back in the war. He says he can hear women and children screaming for their lives. Sometimes, when he sees cars coming down the way, he runs and starts looking for a place to hide, yelling at the top of his voice, 'They're coming for us! Get down! They're trying to blow us up!' When he first came home, he had terrible nightmares and woke up in cold sweats. But now, he wakes up ready to go to work. He doesn't realize that he doesn't have a job; but that's the last thing he remembers from being at home before the war. It wasn't always good, baby, but God is good. God brought your uncle home to us. Whether his mind is a little changed or not, he's home and we're thankful. That's why I was telling you that regardless of how difficult times got, your grandpa brought the joy out of my heart, come rain or shine. I remember one time when your grandpa was cutting weeds. He was trying to draw water out of the well, but for some strange reason, the water wouldn't come out. I sat on the porch and watched him try and figure out what in the world was happening with that old well. He fiddled around about fifteen minutes or so. I wanted to see what was going on too, so I started walking toward him. Then suddenly, he turned the bucket right over his nose, and the water came bursting out. He jumped back and said, 'Good Lord Almighty, the rapture's here! The rapture's upon us.' I laughed so hard my stomach hurt. I laid in the grass and laughed until I couldn't laugh no more."

"You were rolling in the grass, Grandma?"

"Yes baby, that was in my younger days. Your grandma could roll around like the best of them."

"Oh, Grandma," I smiled.

"But these days I'm staying off the grass, cause grandma got itch. I'm right tired of those mosquitoes and gnats that come out in the heat for standing water."

"What's standing water, Grandma?"

"It's when you leave water in a pail too long and it just stands there looking thirsty, saying, 'Jump in, jump in!'"

"Grandma, you're funny," I giggled.

"Well, that's how your grandpa got me. He was a crack-up, and I had a tickle bone waiting to be tickled. That's why he gave me the nickname, Tickles."

"Tickles? Grandpa calls you Tickles?" I laughed.

"Now, you didn't hear it from me, but your grandma could be a little uptight sometimes--cooking, cleaning, sweeping, and scrubbing--trying to keep my mind off of the war and all. I was always so worried about making sure everything was in order. Don't get me wrong. A little order is good. But if that's all you're thinking about, then you get off balance in life. It's okay to have a little fun with your family and friends. I know you're a little young for all this, and you may not understand what I'm saying, but one day you will. I told your momma and daddy the exact same thing when they were courting. Sometimes life can get a little too serious. Just because we're Christians, doesn't mean we can't enjoy life. Your grandpa knew that. He always knew how to touch my buttons," she giggled.

I got so happy inside when she told me about her buttons, and that my grandpa gave her a nickname.

"To this very day, your grandpa still makes my heart sing when he calls me Tickles. That's how I knew he loved me. He touched my heart with laughter and gave me his very best. And guess what?"

"What, Grandma?"

"There's a special someone who wants to give you His very best, too."

"Who, Grandma, who?"

"That Who is God, baby, our Heavenly Father. For God so loved the world that He gave his only Son, that whoever believes in Him should not die but have eternal life."

"God loves me, Grandma?"

"Yes, child, He does. He loved you enough to give you His very, very best. His best was Jesus Christ. There is no other name greater than the name of Jesus, baby. You remember that."

Oh, that's how you know when someone loves you--when they give you things, and give you a nickname, I thought to myself.

"Oh, okay, Grandma. I understand now."

"That's good, baby. Good night, Little Angel."

"Good night, Grandma."

****

You gone be so happy. Happy you'll be. No other little girl, as special to me. You gone be so happy. Happy you'll be.

"Grandma, Grandma! Someone is trying to get me!"

I cried and screamed until my grandma came running into the room. She tried to calm me down, but I was crying hysterically.

"What's the matter, baby? What's wrong?"

"I had a dream that someone was trying to get me. Somebody was in my bed, and he kept touching me. He was making funny noises, and he smelled bad. I tried to make him leave me alone, but he kept touching me. I don't know what he wanted, Grandma. I don't know what he wanted. Why was he doing that to me? What did he want?" I sobbed.

"Oh baby, it was just a dream. I'm right here. Don't be afraid."

"But Grandma, the big red apple is on the dresser, and the dress is on my bed," I insisted.

"What dress, Carmen? What dress are you talking about?"

"It's right there, Grandma. Can't you see it?" I reached over to show her the dress, but it was gone. "It was right there. I don't know where it is, but the apple is on the dresser," I cried, pointing across the room. My grandma got up to look.

"Carmen, I don't see any red apple. You just had a bad dream, baby. And I know exactly what to do for bad dreams."

"Well I hope so, because it was so scary!" I told her as I nestled in right beside her.

"The first thing we need to do is pray."

"Praying will stop the bad dreams?"

"Oh yes, it most certainly will. Let's pray right now, baby. Dear Lord, we ask You to fill this room with Your presence. We pray that You will come and protect us against any spirit that is not like Yours. We thank You for protecting Carmen and ask that You will give her a peaceful sleep. We also thank You for letting my little angel know that You will always be with her, truly love her, and keep her from harm, in Jesus' name we pray. Amen."

"Amen. Thank you, Grandma, for praying with me. I feel better now."

"Okay, baby. I'm going back to my room now."

"Okay. Grandma. Can I ask you one more thing?"

"Yes, dear."

"Can you sleep with me tonight?"

"I sure can, sweetie."

My Grandma cuddled up beside me and held me until I fell asleep. During the night, I was awakened by the sound of footsteps outside my bedroom door. I turned to tell my grandma, but she had left me all alone. I was instantly struck with fear. The wind started to blow, and the curtains moved back and forth in the breeze. The footsteps became softer until I couldn't hear them anymore. I felt relieved and closed my eyes to go to sleep. Then I heard a tapping sound at my bedroom window. I quickly opened my eyes, afraid of what I might see. My uncle was staring at me through the curtains, holding my new dress. He stuck out his tongue and licked the window seal as he slowly lifted the pane. I shuttered inside, but I stayed completely still. I closed my eyes and shut my mouth just like he told me to. I wish I had told my grandma what he did. Maybe she would have stayed, but I was too afraid.

MENTORSHIP

Carmen's grandma loved God and shared very intimate times with her granddaughter. She tried to teach Carmen how to identify uncontaminated love by her own stories of true love with Carmen's grandfather. She taught Carmen that when someone truly loves you, they desire to know and understand everything about you. Carmen's grandpa could make her grandma laugh through even the most difficult of times. Grandma tried to instill in Carmen that true love will always give the best of itself; just like God did when He gave His only Son to the world. Carmen received a glimpse of God's love from her grandparents, but because of her experience that grandma didn't know about, Carmen could not yet fully understand the lessons of God's love.

Mentorship of young girls and women in this current fast-moving, technologically savvy society requires deeper information about how to evaluate someone's intentions and how to perceive danger. Mothers, grandmothers, and other close women in the family must take the responsibility for the mentorship of young women just as God mentored his only Son. We must not neglect the weak or damaged person. An open, on-going dialogue about family members such as Carmen's' uncle would have kept her from the sexual entrapment and fear that destroyed her childhood. We must strengthen and build up one another. The investment of time and prayer, as well as the utilization of family adult services would have kept Carmen's uncle from a place of isolation which led him to prey on the weak and innocent.

Therefore, encourage (admonish, exhort) one another and edify (strengthen and build up) one another, just as you are doing. 1 Thessalonians 5:11 - (AMP)

Chapter Three

MY NAME IS CARMEN

The light from the sun shone through the window facing my bed, and it was time for me to get up and get ready for school. My grandma had no idea what happened to me the night before, and I was too afraid to tell her. At the tender age of seven my voice was tamed and my mouth was sealed because of what my uncle did to me.

When it was time for breakfast, I heard my grandma singing her favorite gospel hymn, *His Eye is on the Sparrow*. I thought my grandma had the voice of an angel, and I loved to hear her sing. Singing and cooking were two of grandma's favorite things to do, along with testifying about the goodness of the Lord.

"Cooking is good for the soul, and singing is good for the heart. For a merry heart doeth good like medicine," she would say.

I could hear the grease popping from the bacon cooking. I could smell the aroma of the cinnamon toast as my grandma poured the milk from the pitcher and stirred the chocolate in, like she usually did. Every time I heard her stirring the chocolate milk with the big brown spoon, I knew she would be calling me soon.

"Carmen, it's time for breakfast."

I slowly opened my bedroom door to see who was in the kitchen. My uncle was already sitting at the table, and he saw me peek out of the door.

He grunted. "How'd you sleep?"

"Fine!" I quickly answered.

Then I went to wash up for breakfast. My grandma called me again.

"Carmen, your food is going to get cold. Hurry up and wash up so you can eat!"

"I'm coming, Grandma."

I finished washing up. I walked into the kitchen and started to sit next to Gary, but my uncle pointed his finger at the chair he wanted me to sit in, right next to him. After I sat down, he put his hand up my dress under the table.

"You know I love you, Carmen, don't you?" he asked me quietly while answering his own question by nodding his head up and down--yes.

I was so afraid of his mean eyes that I nodded my head too, and said, "Yes, Uncle, I do."

"I want you to have a good day at school now, you hear!"

"Yes, sir," I answered, feeling my body starting to tremble. My breakfast didn't taste so good anymore.

"Enjoy your breakfast and have fun at school with your friends," he winked. "See you later, Mom. I'm going to work now."

"Okay, son, you have a good day."

My uncle went back to his room like he always did after breakfast. I really didn't understand why, except from what grandma told me. But I was really glad that he was gone, even if it was just in the other room. Then I finished eating my food, and it was time to go.

"C'mon now, sweetie. Hurry up. School will be starting soon, and you don't want to be late."

My grandma made sure we were always on time for everything — church, school, you name it. So off to school I went. When my school bus dropped me off at school, I got out of the bus and started to sing. *"I'm special, special. My Uncle's special niece. I'm special, special I am."*

A very mean boy ran up to me and started teasing me. "Hey, what you singing?" He looked at me really mean and laughed. "You ain't special. You're skinny, black, and ugly! What makes you think you're special? Yeah, right! Your name is Carmen, you hear me? I said, do you hear me? Your name is Carmen. You're not special. Now answer me!"

I was so afraid I couldn't say anything. Then another little boy ran up to me and started yelling. "What's wrong with you? Don't you know what your name is? What are you, deaf and dumb? Don't you know what your parents named you? Is your name Carmen?"

I looked at them and wondered, why are they picking on me and being so mean? I tried to ignore them by starting to sing again, but I started to stutter instead. "My name is...my name is...." They were laughing and pointing their fingers in my face.

"She talks like she's slow. Look at her. She's black, ugly, and stupid."

I wanted to cry, but then I remembered that I was a big girl now. I couldn't let them see me cry, so I held back my tears.

Mrs. Brown, our teacher, came over and told the boys it wasn't nice to tease others.

"We're not teasing her, Mrs. Brown, honest."

The two boys had big, innocent looking smiles on their faces, even though they weren't telling the truth. I didn't understand why they were treating me so mean. Why would they say that I wasn't special? I wondered. My uncle said that I was his special niece and I believed him because he loved me, but they didn't.

Mrs. Brown told us to all line up and walk quietly into class. Some of the girls in line looked at me funny, and the boys were still laughing at me behind Mrs. Brown's back.

"Students, remember what I said. You are not to tease one another," Mrs. Brown said sternly as we entered the classroom. The boys finally stopped laughing at me.

"Okay, Mrs. Brown," they replied.

We all sat down at our desks as Mrs. Brown wrote something on the chalkboard, then turned and said, "Students, here is your assignment for today. I have a special project for the whole class. I want each of you to create a story, and then read it to the whole class."

The two boys who were teasing me started throwing paper balls across the room, and some of them landed by Mrs. Brown's foot.

"Boys, am I going to have to contact your parents today?"

"No Mrs. Brown," they responded.

"Then I suggest you pay attention so you'll know what your assignment is. Now come and pick up these little paper balls off the floor."

"Yes, Mrs. Brown," they mumbled, easing out from behind their desks.

"Now, as I was saying, each of you is required to write a story that you will read to the class today."

I stared at the chalkboard in disbelief. I didn't want to do it. I was afraid to stand in front of the class. I knew everyone would laugh at me. I quickly put my head down, hoping Mrs. Brown wouldn't notice.

"Carmen, hold your head up. There is no reason for you to put your head down on the desk."

"But Mrs. Brown, I don't know how to write well."

"Carmen, don't worry. I'm going to assign a study buddy for you."

"What's a study buddy?"

"A study buddy will help you with things you have a hard time with, and you can also help him or her."

"I'd rather have a girl study buddy," I requested.

"Okay, Carmen." Mrs. Brown was nice to me. Not only would I have a study buddy, but I would have a new friend at school to play with. I was starting to feel a little better, until one of the boys who was teasing me started whispering to another boy.

"See, even the teacher calls her Carmen. She's stupid!"

The bell rang, and it was lunch time. I didn't want to be around the other kids because they were so mean to me. I didn't want to talk to anyone, not even to Mrs. Brown. I sat at a table by myself while the other kids played. They were having so much fun with each other; but then they would look at me and start laughing. I wished I was invisible, but I knew they could see me. I wanted to go back to my grandma's house. I couldn't wait for the bus to come and pick me up and take me back. When the bell rang again, Mrs. Brown called us back to class.

"It's time to head back inside. Everyone please line up and walk quietly back in. Once you have all settled down, I'll let you know who your study buddy is."

I was so excited that I could hardly sit still as she started to call off names. I began to get even more antsy, because I knew I would have a new friend soon. Then all of a sudden Mrs. Brown said my name, "Carmen."

"Yes, Mrs. Brown!" I said with excitement.

"Your study buddy is Lisa."

I thought to myself, surely this must be a mistake. Lisa is a pretty girl, and everybody likes her; so I didn't move an inch. When I didn't respond, Mrs. Brown repeated my name.

"Carmen, your study buddy is Lisa. The two of you are going to make a great team. Now it's time for everyone to get started on your stories."

"Mrs. Brown, can I write about all the surprises that my uncle gave me?" I asked.

"Of course, Carmen. You can write about whatever you would like."

"Okay, Mrs. Brown."

I started writing about the big red apple, my pretty new dress with the bow, and the ice cream surprise my uncle gave me. I made sure I didn't write about him touching me, because I was afraid my uncle would hurt me more. Then I got stuck and Lisa started helping me. She was really nice to me, and she was very pretty. I noticed her skin was almost white, and her hair was long and straight. I started thinking that's why so many people liked her. I was glad that she was my new friend. Before I knew it, class was almost over and Mrs. Brown was erasing the assignment off the chalkboard.

"Students, class is about to end. Gather your things and make sure that you keep your stories to read another day."

I was so glad I didn't have to read my story out loud. I put it in my jacket pocket, got up from my desk and started walking out of the classroom with my head down. Mrs. Brown walked over to me and gently lifted my chin with her hand.

"Carmen, remember to hold your head up. There's no reason for you to put your head down."

"Yes, Mrs. Brown. I forgot," I said walking out the door with my head up if only for a moment.

I knew that when I got to my grandma's house my uncle would be waiting for me with another surprise. My grandma told me that my uncle loved me, but something felt wrong about what he did to me. He called me his special niece, but I didn't really feel special. All the kids at school were mean to me. I started to wonder if I was special at all. If my uncle didn't love me, why did he give me the ice cream surprise, the pretty new dress, and the big red apple? Why did he? I wondered. One thing I did know. My name was Carmen.

PURPOSE

The name Carmen has significant meaning, just like your name does. Carmen means *'joy'*. She had already been through very difficult times in her young life, but the name her mother and father had given her surpassed the challenges she faced. Carmen had an inner strength, even as a child. When she became an adult, her spirit could not help but express the nature of the call of God in her life.

Do you know what your name means? If you don't know, begin to search out what the true meaning of your name is. When your parents named you, they did not make a mistake. They were just vessels whom God used to bring your gift to the world. What gift is in you? Your name will reveal the purpose for which God created you.

God created me so I can be a gift to the world and deliver a message of healing and deliverance to others from my own personal experiences. It is my desire to teach mothers and concerned family members on how to protect their young children through open dialogue and complete transparency about the sinful nature of mankind and the issues of life. When God created me, He had a purpose in mind for me to fulfill. The name I received from my parents was in line with that purpose. I have continued to follow God's plan of touching lives and winning souls for the Kingdom of God, even through difficult times in my life. I want every individual who has ever experienced similar sexual trauma to know that you too can overcome the ugly experiences and debilitating memories. God wants you to *thrive* in life, not just *survive*.

For I know the plans I have for you," declares the LORD, "plans to prosper you and not to harm you, plans to give you hope and a future." Jeremiah 29:11 - (NKJV)

Chapter Four

ACCEPTANCE

"Carmen!" my grandma called. "Carmen, your momma is here to pick you, your sister, and brothers up. It's time to go home."

I went into the living room. I was so happy to see my momma. I couldn't wait to go home. I knew I would be safe there, or at least I thought I would be.

"Carmen, get your bags," my momma said.

I went back to the room and picked up my bags. When I walked out the door, my uncle put his hand over his mouth and pointed to me. I was so scared that I dropped my bags, and my momma heard the commotion.

"Carmen, what's taking you so long? Hurry up so we can go."

I picked up my bags and slowly walked down the hall. I could feel my uncle staring at me, but I kept walking toward my momma.

"Where is your sister and brothers?" she asked.

"They're in the backyard playing."

"Okay, let's go get them so we can all go home."

We all scrambled into the car to go home. It was a long ride to the house, and before we knew it, Gary was snoring in the front seat. Trease and I sang *Itsy Bitsy Spider* along the way. I was so happy that I didn't have to worry about my uncle anymore. I was glad that we lived so far away, and that my uncle couldn't drive because of what happened to him in the war.

Once we got home, my sister could barely wait to jump out of the car to go play on the swing. She started talking so loudly that Gary woke up.

"Momma, can I play on the swing? Please, can I?"

"Trease, you know the routine. It's time to go in the house."

"Oh, Momma," Trease replied.

"Be obedient, Trease, and let's go inside."

We all got out of the car and Gary started to head toward the house. We could tell that he was still sleepy because he was moving slower than a turtle.

"Now you know that boy is tired from playing so hard because he never walks that slow," my momma said as Gary dragged his feet walking in front of us. Trease was tugging on momma's dress because she still wanted to play in the yard.

"Oh Momma, can't I just play a little more?" she whined.

"If you don't stop that whining, I got something for you!"

"Oh, okay," she pouted and took momma's hand into the house. Gary went straight to his room and closed the door behind him. Trease started to follow him, but then went to our room to play.

"I guess it's just you and me," momma said. "How was your stay at your grandma's house?"

"It was okay," I sighed.

"Is that all you have to say? You're usually a little chattier than that. What did you do while you were at your grandma's house?"

"We all played on the swing, and then Uncle came outside while I was on the swing."

"Well, that's nice to hear, being that he's been keeping pretty much to himself since his injury from the war. It's good to hear that he's finally acting more like himself."

"He even brought me a really pretty new dress with a bow, and we had an ice cream party."

"Really?"

"Yep, and he also gave me a big red apple. He said that I was his special niece and we laughed and played in his room.

"His special niece?" she questioned. "It sounds like you had fun. Did your sister get to play too?"

"No. It was just me and Uncle," I shouted with a very loud voice.

"Okay, okay, calm down. I certainly know what it's like when you get pretty new dresses."

"You do?" I asked, surprised to hear her say this.

"I most certainly do. Only big girls get special gifts."

As soon as she said that I knew for sure that my uncle really did love me.

"Did you tell your uncle thank you?" she asked.

I didn't say anything at first.

"Carmen, did you tell your uncle thank you?"

"Yes, I did," I said, then hesitated. "When did you become special, Momma?"

"It was a very long time ago, baby. I can hardly remember it."

"Was it when you became a big girl?"

"The only thing I remember is being very excited when my uncle gave me my first pretty new dress, and how it was our little secret. That's all I remember," she said as her eyes welled up with tears. "Well, it's getting late now. Let's take care of your clothes so you can get ready for bed."

I handed her my jacket to hang it up in the closet. She was so tired that she dropped it on the floor. When she reached to pick it up, the paper that I wrote in school dropped right beside her foot. I immediately picked it up, hoping she would not see it, but she did.

"Carmen, what is that?"

"It's my assignment from school today," I said reluctantly.

"Well, don't you want to share it with me?"

"It's about the pretty dress that Uncle gave me."

"Oh, okay. Well, since we're both tired, let's talk about it another time. Okay, baby?"

"Okay. Momma?"

"Yes, dear?"

"When will Daddy be home?"

"He's working late tonight. He'll be home in about an hour."

"Will you give him a kiss for me? Please?" I grinned.

"Yes, I most certainly will. Now go to sleep. Your sister and brothers need to be tucked in too," she said as she kissed me good night.

I wondered why she didn't remember more, but I was so sleepy that I just laid my head down to go to sleep on my pretty pink pillow. I knew I would have chores to do in the morning, and I needed my rest. My momma required me to help her with most of the household chores, including cooking and cleaning up the house. Even though I was a child, I had a lot of responsibilities because I was, after all, the oldest daughter. I was required to go directly home from school. I never played much outside with the other kids. After hearing 'no' so often, I just stopped asking and worked even harder for her approval. I wanted so desperately to please her.

****

With every visit to my grandma's house, my uncle's unwanted touching and physical control became more frequent and intense until the molestation became incest. The more he violated me, the more I would clean up at home to feel better about myself. I started to compensate for his abuse of me with the acceptance of my performance at home. Every time he would force himself upon me, I felt somewhat in control when I cleaned. But it didn't matter how hard I worked to clean.

I couldn't erase the disgusting stench my uncle left behind. I felt empty and began to cling to my father. I felt in my heart that my father loved me. He told me that I could do or be anything I set my mind to, and that all I needed to do was pursue education. I consequently strove to lead a life that was deserving of my father's love. The need for his acceptance created a hidden drive within me that intensified my need to excel and be perfect in everything I did. Mediocrity was not an option--at least not in my world. I had developed a fear that I might be accused of doing something wrong, and that my parents wouldn't believe the truth. My confusion and ambiguous feelings also led me into a state of complete silence about my uncle's sexual entrapment. The only thing left for me to do was to remain silent and try to become the person my father would someday be proud of.

CONFIDENCE

Carmen did not realize she was beautiful and accepted by God. The warped words from her uncle and the ugly things constantly said to her at school re-enforced the negative self-image she had of herself. Therefore, she worked herself to the bone trying to gain the acceptance of her parents.

Have you ever listened to someone who only spoke negative words to you? Have you tried to turn a deaf ear to those words only to find they keep playing back like an automatic recording in your mind? Chances are you have. It is something that happens to all of us, but what can be done about it? The Lord wants you to reprogram your mind by meditating on Scripture to reinforce the truth of God's Word in your life. Also be assured that God will be an ever-present help through the difficult times in your life. You were created as a beautiful and perfect image of who He is. Let your confidence rest on *that!*

Finally, brothers and sisters, whatever is true, whatever is noble, whatever is right, whatever is pure, whatever is lovely, whatever is admirable—if anything is excellent or praiseworthy—think about such things. Philippians 4:8 (NIV)

Chapter Five

IS SILENCE GOLDEN?

Sunny days didn't seem as sunny anymore. Frequently, I reflect on the days when I went outside to play at my grandma's house. I often ponder the day that I became a big girl. I remember when it was just my sister, my brothers, and me taking turns swinging on the swing. We had so much fun, just the four of us. We drank ice cold lemonade and spent time swinging all day. We ran through the grass and looked up towards the big blue sky. We laughed and dreamed together. We were children without a care in the world. But things were different now. My innocence had been taken away, and I could no longer pretend to be invisible. No matter how hard I closed my eyes, I could always feel my uncle's hands violating me. I could smell his scent as he pressed up against me. Many times, I tried to turn my head away from him in disgust. I could still smell his breath against my skin as he breathed heavily and out of control; so I would hold my breath for as long as I could. I learned to turn my feelings off, to feel numb to a part of me that I hated. I hated the part of me that gave into his need to control me through fear and deceit.

Now that I'd been touched as no child should, my mind began to develop in ways that I did not understand. I had been lied to by someone I thought loved and cared for me. Turning my feelings off caused me to develop a shield around my heart to protect me from anything I perceived as bad.

I hated my uncle, and I hated myself because I had a need to be accepted by him through the performance of the things that would satisfy the very essence of his sexual desire. Yet in turn, the very sight and smell of him nauseated me. His abuse of me continued day in and day out. His bed became my bed. I was his little toy to play with at will. Whatever he told me to do, I did. I can still remember the pressure of his hands against my back. He controlled my body and mind by the strength of his weakness and the lies of his tongue. My body had been trained to yield to the sound of his voice. Then one day, my parents decided to move from Mississippi to California.

My beloved father, Leroy Wade, Sr., worked tirelessly to provide for his family. He traveled to California to learn a trade, becoming a plasterer of houses and a cement mason. As he came back and forth from California, the people in the city heard of his ability and great cement work. A white man asked him to do some work for him. My dad told him what the work would cost and the man agreed. After finishing the work, my dad was paid, and the white man said to him, "This is too much money to pay a 'nigger'." He then told my dad, "You better be out of town by tomorrow." That very night my father complied to the man's demand. For our safety, he packed us up and moved us to California. During this time, the Ku Klux Klan was prevalent, and my dad did not want to take the chance of jeopardizing his family.

When we were older, our father told us of the threat on our lives that prompted the hasty move.

In those times children were to be seen and not heard. We were not told things we needed to know. My mom didn't even tell me about menstruation and what would happen if certain things occurred. That's just how it was! Because of this communication dynamic in my family, I failed to reveal and deal with the reality of being sexually abused by my uncle. I had not dealt with my abuse openly with my family, so it was just a matter of time before the past would repeat itself in a completely different form. This time, however, everyone would know the secret shame of my youth.

COMMUNICATION

There is a saying that "silence is golden," but is it really? Keeping a confidence is one thing but remaining silent about something that can change another person's life is selfish. Carmen had no idea what was happening to her. She was ignorant about human growth and sexual development. Her parents hadn't shared that aspect of life with her. Therefore, she was in the dark and alone. She had no idea where to turn, which is a dangerous place to be.

It is very important for us to communicate with our children, regardless of how difficult or uncomfortable the topic may be. Do not be afraid to talk to your children about anything that may be on their minds. Failure to talk openly about sensitive issues leaves the door open for your children to learn wrong principles from their schools, social media, or their peers. Our children need our encouragement, hope, and help until they have developed the right life-sustainable skills.

As a typical child, Carmen had a trusting nature. However, she had low self-esteem, a lack of knowledge about sexual development and reproduction, and a fear of open dialogue on any subject with her parents. These deficiencies made her very vulnerable to sinful and ignorant people. Carmen, her brother, and her uncle suffered because responsible family members did not direct them on the right path by setting an example of openness and intelligence.

Do not be fooled. Your children are waiting for you to talk to them. If you share necessary facts without any judgment toward the questions they ask, they will listen to what you have to say. Transparency and truth are always the key to an open relationship with the young as well as the seasoned.

Direct your children onto the right path, and when they are older, they will not leave it. Proverbs 22:6 - (NLT)

Chapter Six

NIGHTMARE RE-LIVED

When I became a teenager, I thought I knew a few things. However, what I knew did not include the mind of a teenage boy. One weekend, my parents took a flight to Los Angeles. They left my brother Gary in charge. The next morning, I went to my girlfriend Whitney's house. Whitney was adventurous and fun to be around, but being teenagers, we quickly got bored at her house and went back to mine. When we arrived at my house, my brother's two friends, Jason and Joe were there talking about their favorite basketball team. Gary had left to get some burgers from the diner. Suddenly, Whitney began to laugh like a little girl. "What's so funny?" I asked. "Stop being so sensitive. Nobody's talking about you," Joe said, and he began whispering in Whitney's ear. She shook her head in agreement to whatever he was saying. I knew that she was a little adventurous, but I didn't know how much until she went upstairs with Joe. "We'll see you guys later," Whitney laughed. I just stared at her and Joe as they closed the door behind them.

When I turned around, I became nervous as I saw the look in Jason's eyes. I acted like I didn't see him and pretended he wasn't even there. He made sure I knew he was in the room.

"Hey, Carmen. How you been doing?" he asked.

"Fine, I guess," I answered, trying to nonchalantly shrug the question off.

"Carmen, why you acting so shy, girl? You ain't that shy."

All I could think of while he was talking was how nervous I was being in a room with him all alone. Before I knew it, he grabbed my arm and pulled me toward him.

"Come over here for a minute. I have a surprise for you."

His word choice brought ugly thoughts into my head, so when I moved, I inched toward him like a sheep to a wolf. I was a fifteen-year-old girl that had a learned helplessness in resisting what I knew was wrong. Therefore, I continued to move in his direction. The closer I got to him, the more I felt like I should run away; but the behavioral habits ingrained in me unconsciously took over, regardless of what I wanted. The sound of his voice made me feel as if I was under a spell as he began to whisper in my ear.

"You know Carmen, I've always thought you were special. I get excited every time I see your pretty eyes and your chocolate brown skin. You're not like the other girls. There's something special about you. I've always liked how tall you are, and I love the way you walk. But there's even something more special about you."

"Really?"

"Yeah, girl, you know what I'm sayin'!"

He laughed and kissed me on the cheek. He then placed his lips against mine and entered my mouth. I was shocked and taken aback as his tongue invoked a feeling of intrusion within me;

but I conformed to his advances out of fear of what he would do if I rejected him.

"You know I wouldn't hurt you, right?" he asked, pressing his body up against mine. Inwardly, I knew what he was thinking, but I was afraid to resist.

"I don't think," I answered, almost robotically, but he didn't notice.

"You know you like it when I kiss you, don't you?" he said, breathing heavily as the tone of his voice became increasingly familiar.

I had an immediate flash back to when I heard those exact same words, and I became afraid all over again. I wanted to run, but out of terror I remained still, repeating what he wanted to hear.

"Yes, I do," I said, not knowing what was about to happen to me. My parents never talked to me about what happens between teenage boys and girls. It was a closed subject in my house. However, Jason knew exactly what he was doing. It was a rude awakening that would rock my world for the rest of my life.

"Carmen, did you know that I was raised without a father? He was the only one I could really talk to. He understood me. I just need someone who understands me like he did. You know, someone that gets me."

"What do you mean, 'someone who gets you?'" I asked.

"You know, someone who understands the real me, and that someone is you. I can always talk to you. That's what's special about you. I always have your ear. You listen to me, and you don't judge me--not like my momma. I can tell you anything, and I know you won't say a word. I just want us to be together, so I can be a part of you and you can be a part of me. Nobody has to know."

"What exactly are you saying?" I asked, starting to feel uncomfortable once again.

"Well...your brother's gone, and your parents aren't here. So now's the perfect time," he said, nuzzling up against me.

"Perfect time for what?" I asked him innocently.

All of a sudden, he kissed me again and started applying pressure to my waist with his hands, causing my knees to buckle until I could no longer stand.

"Jason, stop!" I said firmly, almost proud of the words that came from my mouth.

"Say my name again!" he commanded.

"Jason, please, you have to stop!" I begged, as his grip on me became even more intense.

"I like it when you say my name," he whispered, breathing heavily with an evil tone, obviously enjoying himself.

"Jason, Gary will be back any minute," I yelled, hoping he would stop and trying to break free at the same time. He acted like he didn't hear me and started whispering words in my ear that made me tremble inside.

"Don't tell anyone. It's our little secret."

Following through on the words he spoke in a whisper he began to forcibly rape me against my will.

"Jason," I protested. "Please, don't do this," I pleaded; but he refused to stop and demanded my silence.

"Shut up and give me what I want!" he ordered, slamming me against the floor and ripping my underwear off, brutally violating me as if my voice had no sound. Tears ran down my face and I began to sob in despair.

"Yeah, that's what I like to hear. That's what I want. Yeah . . . give it to me! Give it all to me," he breathed heavily and out of control, rising up within me and ripping my insides. He yanked my body off the floor and turned me around. Gripping my backside, he repetitively pounded his flesh into mine. I could feel myself bleeding, and I bit my lip in pain. He pushed me down, and I tried to crawl away; but he grabbed me again and flipped me over like a rag doll and continued to rape me. I cried out when I heard the upstairs door open, but then it shut.

"I said be quiet! They'll hear you," he demanded, gripping my neck in his hands. In fear, I silenced myself. He raised my legs and forcefully caused my body to rise off the floor and my flesh to tear as he relieved himself within me. To him I was an invisible release, and the sound of my voice was no different than the sound of the wind. When he called my name, fear silenced me.

"Carmen..." I turned my head and shut my mouth just as I had been conditioned to do. Besides, it was our little secret. He didn't have to worry about me saying a thing; but there would be another voice that would one day speak...loud and clear.

RAPE

A teenage boy was able to whisper sweet words in Carmen's ear to submit her to what he wanted. After he forcibly raped her and silenced what voice she had left, she ended up in a state of shame with even lower self-esteem and more challenges. Her childhood experiences had come back to haunt her through another selfish act of manipulation and control.

Carmen was wrestling with inner self-hatred. The negative things continually said to her by her peers put deep imprints on her soul and mind. She began to believe that she was 'big, black, and ugly.' Therefore, she could not ingest the good things said about her. When the rape happened, it re-enforced her self-hatred. She could not forgive herself for what happened to her; and yet, the guilt was not hers to forgive.

Are you holding onto something that is not yours to forgive? Has someone abused you, and you have taken the burden of that abuse as if it was your fault? You do not have to bear that burden any longer. It is up to you to release the cause and effect and then carry the crimes done against you to Jesus. Unresolved negative feelings become a toxin to your spirit that, if left undealt with, will eventually erode the good things God has planted and is trying to develop in you. The enemy's plan is to take even the most diligently faithful to God out of purpose...and out of this earth. Self-hatred is an invitation for a spirit of self-destruction and even suicide to enter your mind. You have great worth. Believe what the Word of God says about you. Ultimately,

Carmen found that God would have the final say in her life.

Come to Me, all you who labor and are heavy-laden and overburdened, and I will cause you to rest. I will ease and relieve and refresh your souls. Matthew 11:28 – (AMP)

Chapter Seven

WORMS

The continual confusion that swirled in my mind about all that had happened to me started with the secret code of silence that existed at my house around the subject of "sex". Even though I was in the tenth grade, I didn't know anything about where babies came from. I didn't even know anything about a woman's monthly cycle before it happened to me.

One afternoon I was on a swing at the park and fell off. When I got up from the ground, I saw blood on my skirt. I walked home as fast as I could and told my momma. I was hysterical.

"Momma, I'm bleeding. Something's wrong," I cried, pointing to the stains on my dress.

"That's just your monthly," she said. "I'll show you what to do before you ruin your clothes."

What does monthly mean? I thought to myself. I had no idea whatsoever. Although I didn't understand, it was somehow obvious that I wasn't to ask her any more questions about it. I simply did as she said. I didn't really understand any more than that until the following month when it happened again. However, I noticed it seemed to eventually run its course and then stop. I didn't think about it again until my sister and I went to visit my aunt in Seattle, Washington. Suddenly I realized that I did not have a monthly anymore and thought it was all over.

"Hey Trease, do I look fat?" I asked.

"Well, you do look like you're starting to eat a little too much."

"What do you mean, eat too much?"

"Well, you asked me!"

"I know, but seriously, do I look like something's wrong with me? I look the same everywhere else, except here," pointing to my stomach.

"Well, it does look a little fat," Trease agreed.

"Momma gave me some medication for worms. Maybe they're just moving around. I don't know. Let me see your stomach," I said.

Trease lifted her shirt, and I felt her stomach. It didn't feel hard like mine.

"Feel my stomach. It feels different than yours," I said. I lifted my shirt a little and she gently placed her hand on my belly.

"Oh wow, you're right! It does feel hard. You must really be infested with worms! Lift up your shirt higher so I can see."

I lifted my shirt a little higher this time. Suddenly her eyes got really big!

"Girl, you look like you've got a bowling ball in there! You're not kidding. Have you been trying to hide your stomach? Why didn't you say something sooner? Something could be really wrong with you. You could be really sick with worms, Carmen."

I had been conditioned to keep my mouth shut about almost everything, so my sister and I didn't have a clue about what was happening to me. We started looking through my aunt's books that she had at her house. Trease pulled out an interesting looking book. It had a picture of a man kissing a woman.

"Here's a book on love," she smiled.

"We don't need that one," I quickly insisted. "Put that back."

"How do you know? We haven't even read the table of contents yet."

"I just know. That's not it! I yelled.

"What?" she asked looking perplexed.

"How could love make my stomach big? What is love? Look again."

"Okay, well here's another one. The title is *He Touched Me.*"

We both laughed and then composed ourselves.

"Trease, that's not going to help. Keep looking. There's got to be something here somewhere."

"Okay, I've got one."

"What did you find?"

"It's a book titled, *The Key to Culture*, by Paul L. Gilbert," Trease said.

"Read the table of contents."

"There's something here about introductions."

"What do introductions have to do with my stomach?" I asked.

"You never know. Let's just read it."

"Okay, go ahead. It can't hurt."

"Introductions, Cards, Mastery of Conversation, Dinners, Table Manners, Finger Foods, Silver Service, Receptions."

"What are finger foods?" I asked.

"Who are you asking?"

"You! Just keep reading."

"Weddings, Wedding Anniversaries, Balls and Dances."

"Balls and Dances? Put that book away. Auntie would have a fit if she knew we were looking at that. Find another book," I said.

"Here's another one. It's titled, *A Bell for Adano,* by John Heresy."

"No, that won't help. That's the World War II novel that Aunt Bell is always talking about. One day, I'm going to read that book. She keeps telling me how good it is."

"You're going to read a book with 269 pages? Yeah, right!" Trease scoffed.

"C'mon, Trease. Stop playing. This is serious. Keep looking. I'm sure there's a book here somewhere that can help."

"Okay, okay."

We continued to look for what seemed like hours. Finally, Trease found a book that peaked my interest.

"Here's a medical book, Carmen."

"Great. Let me see it."

She handed me the book, and I flipped through the pages until I found the table of contents; but I didn't see anything helpful, so I turned to the back of the book and found the index.

"Here are two words that sound familiar," I said hopefully.

"What are they?"

"Monthly cycle."

"What does that mean?" Trease asked.

"I don't have a clue. The meaning has to be here somewhere," I sighed, flipping to the page number, hoping to find the answer. "Here it is. *'Menstruation, a recurring monthly series of changes in women in which an egg is produced in the process known as ovulation.'"*

"Ovula . . . what?"

"Be quiet and let me finish reading." I was impatient. 'The uterine lining thickens to allow for implantation if fertilization occurs. If the egg is not fertilized...'"

"What egg? And why are we talking about fertilization? You haven't been in the grass, have you?"

"Trease, no!"

"I'm just saying...I'm really confused about what you're saying. I don't understand a word you're reading, and besides, it won't help us because we're not women. We're just kids!"

"Just let me finish! 'The woman's lining of her uterus breaks down and is discharged during menstruation.'"

"Discharged? What does that mean?" Trease asked, increasingly confused.

"I don't know! I'm not a woman, so it can't be talking about me."

"Well, something is wrong. Your stomach is really big, sis."

"I know. I'm really scared."

"What are we going to do? Who can we tell?" Trease was worried now.

"We can't tell anybody. Let's just hope my stomach gets smaller again by itself."

"Okay, whatever you say," she shrugged.

"Let's go in the kitchen and get something to eat," I suggested.

"Did Aunt Bell buy the ice cream she said she was going to get?"

"Let's go see."

We went into the kitchen and opened the refrigerator.

"Great, there it is. Sit down and I'll make you a bowl," I offered.

I opened the bucket of vanilla ice cream and instantly heard my uncle's voice, *"You gone be so happy. Happy you'll be. No other niece, as special to me. You gone be so happy. Happy you'll be."* I stood still and couldn't move an inch until I heard my sister's voice.

"Why are you standing there like that? What are you doing?" asked Trease.

"Huh? Oh. I don't know. I guess I was just thinking about something."

"Well, can you scoop and think at the same time? I want some ice cream."

"Ha! Ha! Trease. Very funny."

I turned my attention back to scooping the ice cream in her bowl and then in mine. I sat down to eat it, but I couldn't enjoy it because of the old memories that played back in my mind. Still, I tried to pretend that everything was okay because I didn't want my sister to ask me what I was thinking about. I just bit into my ice cream like I normally did.

TRANSPARENCY

Carmen's childhood questions could have been answered and her fears silenced if transparency had existed in her family. So many of the problems of her generation could have been avoided if hers was a generation of open communication and honesty.

We must not think that silence about all-important issues is protecting our children. It will eventually erode the family structure and cause children to close up and internalize their questions, pains, and fears. In frustration, they will go outside to get answers from their peers or other potentially dangerous sources. Furthermore, the danger of closed communication in the home is that there is always a breaking point. There will always come a negative bursting out that can actually kill the parent-to-child relationship.

The real protection of our children is in open discussion about experiences and lessons we as parents have learned through difficult or uncertain times in our lives. They must know that what they are going through is not isolated *just* to them. They need to be assured they are not *abnormal* because they have questions, fears, and uncertainties. We can bridge rather than cause a deeper chasm in the generation gap that still exists in our culture today through transparency and humility, salted with love and grace, and frosted with the sweetness of the Word of God.

An honest answer is like a kiss on the lips. Proverbs 24:26 - (NIV)

Chapter Eight

ANOTHER SURPRISE

"Ouch!" I cried.

"What's wrong?" asked Trease.

"My tooth hurts. This ice cream is really cold."

"It's always really cold."

"This time something's different," I grimaced.

"It's the same ice cream we always have," she said.

"I know. Maybe the pain will stop soon. I don't want any more ice cream."

"Can I have the rest of yours?"

"Sure, go ahead," I offered. "I can't eat it."

My tooth continued to hurt for the rest of the day and throughout the night, so Aunt Bell took me to the dentist the next morning. After the dentist examined me, he recommended that my aunt take me to see a medical doctor. Although she was worried, she tried not to show it on her face as she drove us back to her house. Upon arriving, Trease was waiting to see what happened. She ran to the car and started asking questions right away.

"What happened? What did the dentist say?"

"He told Aunt Bell to take me to a medical doctor."

"Why? What's wrong with you?" She asked, half panicking.

"I don't know, and my tooth still hurts," I groaned.

Aunt Bell told me to go inside so she could give me something to stop my tooth from hurting. She gave me some Tylenol to stop the pain. Once my tooth felt a little better I fell asleep. I didn't wake until the next morning when my aunt came into the room where I was sleeping.

"Carmen, I need you to get up now and get dressed. It's time to go to the doctor."

"Okay, Aunt Bell," I answered obediently.

"How is your tooth feeling?"

I rubbed my cheek and squinted my eyes.

"Oooh...it still hurts."

"Here's some Orajel to make it feel better. Rub it on your tooth and gums before you brush your teeth. Then wait a few minutes until your gums feel numb. It will help to take the pain away."

"What is Orajel, Aunt Bell?"

"It's something that will numb your gums so that the aching will go away. Now go ahead and rub it on your gums."

I got up and went to the bathroom to get cleaned up. Then it was time to go to the doctor. I walked slowly out the front door because I was afraid. At least the pain had stopped, and my tooth didn't hurt any more. My aunt prayed all the way to the doctor's office. It comforted me to hear her praying, "Dear Lord, we thank you that You're in control and that You will be glorified in Carmen's life. Help her to be strong. Help us all." She began to hum. I felt like God was sitting right next to me. It's hard to explain, but I just knew in my heart that God was right there in the car with us.

We arrived at the doctor's office and went inside. The nurse asked us to be seated. As I sat down, my aunt immediately started pacing the floor. I wondered what the dentist had told her. She never stopped praying, at least while I was in the room. Then the nurse called from behind the big glass window.

"Carmen, the doctor can see you now."

I went in to see the doctor, and he examined me. After he was done, he instructed the nurse to have my aunt come into the room. I'll never forget the glare in his eyes as he looked at me from across the table. I felt ashamed, but I didn't know why. I just put my head down like I always did when I felt embarrassed or helpless. My aunt opened the door and saw me with my head down.

"Carmen, what's wrong? Why are you holding your head down like that? What is it doctor? What is going on?"

"Mrs. Bell, I need you to sit down for a moment," he said, motioning toward a chair.

My aunt looked at the doctor with tears in her eyes. I could see she became even more concerned when he asked her to sit down. She sat down after taking a deep breath.

"Mrs. Bell, there's no easy way to say this, so I'll just say it. Your niece is pregnant."

"Pregnant! Surely there must be a mistake! She's a quiet, sweet girl. There's no way she could be pregnant!"

It was nice to hear her say that I was sweet.

"Well, she is indeed pregnant. Seven months pregnant."

"Oh my God!" she gasped.

That's when yet another nightmare began. I thought to myself, *"Pregnant?!* But I'm not a woman yet. How did I get pregnant? My momma is going to kill me!"

We all left the room, and my aunt took my hand, but she didn't say a word to me until we got to her house. I think she was just as shocked as I was, if not more. It was a long silent ride all the way back. I didn't know what to say or think. I just sat in the car, silently crying until there were no more tears left to cry.

When we got back to my aunt's house, Trease was anxiously waiting to see what the doctor said, but this time she was waiting on the porch. I got out of the car and walked toward her. She could tell the news wasn't good. I had been crying almost the entire way. My eyes were puffy, and my nose was swollen from blowing it so much. I had a big wad of tissue in one hand, and I was wiping my tears with the other. Trease ran off the porch and hugged me really tight.

"What's wrong? What happened? What did the doctor say?"

I could hardly get the words out because I started crying again.

"He said I'm pregnant."

"Pregnant?"

"Yes, pregnant!"

"With a baby? How'd that happen?" Trease asked, surprised and confused.

"Come inside girls," my aunt whispered. "We don't want the neighbors to start gossiping."

But it was already too late. The neighbors heard us talking outside. I could feel their eyes watching us, and my heart sank with embarrassment. My aunt looked at the shame in my eyes. She took both our hands, and we all went inside.

"Carmen, never mind about the neighbors. They're always looking for something to gossip about. I know you're scared right now, but everything will work out."

"How can you be so sure?" I asked her, feeling so alone and frightened.

"Sometimes things happen to us that we don't always have an answer for."

"Well, I don't have any answers about what is happening to me!"

"Would you like to go to church with me tonight? Maybe you'll get some answers to your questions there, or at least answers to your prayers."

"Yes, I would. But, what about Trease?"

Trease had gone into one of the bedrooms and was pacing back and forth. I could hear her through the door.

"Lord, we need...we need some help! If you don't help us, no one can. Lord, do you hear me up there? Do you hear me talking to you? Sometimes I wonder if you even listen to me. Why would you let something like this happen? We are just kids, Lord. We're just kids! We don't know what we're doing. Can you hear my voice, Lord? I hope You can, 'cause we really need some help!"

She must have remembered the many times momma prayed for us because she sounded just like her.

"Trease, do you want to go to church with Carmen and me tonight?" my aunt asked.

"Yes, I do. I need some answers *tonight!*" Trease said anxiously, bursting into the room to join us.

"Then let's get ready to go to church."

When we arrived at the church, the choir was singing a beautiful song. We all sat down on the pew. I forgot about my situation for a while. As the choir sang, I could hear my mother's words, "If you pray, the Lord will hear you, and I declare, He will make a way." I started to pray the only way that I knew how, because I didn't really know God very well. I knew I needed help, so I started praying with everything I had.

"God, my momma said if I would pray, that You would hear me. She said that You would make a way."

I prayed until the tears streamed down my face, and I could barely see in front of me. The next thing I knew, I was praying what the choir was singing. *"Lord, if you make a way for me, I will serve You for the rest of my life. For the rest of my life Lord, I will serve You!"* I was praying so loud that it felt like I was the only person in the church. I could hear myself praying, and it sounded like an angel was praying with me. I closed my eyes and lifted my hands while crying out to the Lord. All of a sudden I opened my eyes. The lady singing was looking right at me. *"Lord, if You make a way for her, she will serve You. She will serve You for the rest of her life. Lord, if You make a way for her, she will serve You. She will love You for the rest of her life. Lord, make a way. Make a way for her right now."* The whole choir joined in. I started crying even harder, but this time it was different. It was a cry of joy because I knew that God had heard my prayer. Even though I was too young to understand that I was making a vow to the Lord, it didn't matter in that moment because I needed Him just the same. I felt the presence of God like I had never felt it before. However, my mind would not let me rest during the night because I knew I would have to face my momma. I was so afraid of what would happen when she arrived because she was always so strict with me. To my surprise, she was kind to me when she arrived. She didn't react like I thought she would. She started asking me about the baby's father in a calm voice.

"Carmen, I want you to know that I love you."

I looked at my momma for the first time in a different light as she continued to speak. Regardless of the words that came out of her mouth, I still had an inward fear to speak out about anything. I just listened to her go on and on about what she was going to do.

"I understand that young girls can be carried away by their emotions," she began, "and it's easy to be tricked into doing something that you did not plan. I was young once too. I just wish I had talked to you about this before. Your heart was obviously caught up, and this is the result."

My momma had it all figured out in her head, and I dare not interrupt her. She didn't know that Jason forced himself upon me or that when I told him to stop, he refused. My heart had nothing to do with it. I was afraid of her, so I just listened to her speak. I just kept my mouth shut because of the fear that my uncle had first instilled in me. I don't know what she would have done if she knew what really happened.

"What is the name of the baby's father?" she asked.

Since it was a secret, I lied to her out of fear of what Jason would do to me if I told her the truth.

"His name is John, but I don't know where he is. I heard that his family moved away."

"You haven't seen him in seven months?" she asked with a perplexed look on her face.

I shrugged my shoulders and shook my head, "No Momma, I haven't," hoping she would believe me. But I had seen Jason just a few weeks before at the corner store, and he rejected me with cruel words. He told me I was a black tramp.

"Carmen, you're too young to raise a baby. It would be a terrible strain at your age. I'm going to take care of everything. There are organizations that will take care of you and your baby. You'll be able to stay with them until the baby is delivered. Once you have the baby, you will have to give it up for adoption and that's that! But before I take you, we'll have to visit your school and tell the principal that you will not be returning," she adamantly said.

My heart sank because I had dreams of finishing school to become a nurse. I had a need to take care of young children so they would be protected from harm. I didn't want what happened to me to happen to them. However, my momma had no idea what my dreams were because I didn't talk unless I was forced to. Her controlling nature always won out. I just listened to her and did what she said.

"When we get back home I don't know how your father is going to react about your pregnancy; but I'm going to schedule an appointment for us to see your principal about your schooling."

My momma was determined. We packed up our bags and left the next morning. Upon our arrival, my father was standing on the porch waiting for us. I hesitated for a minute. I was so afraid of what he might say to me, but he just looked at me with disappointment in his eyes. Then he spoke the most painful words I'd ever heard him say.

"From this day forward, I have nothing to say to you. You are not to speak to me, and I do not expect to hear your voice."

I was looking for support and received rejection instead. I was an unwed, pregnant, sixteen-year-old girl, and an embarrassment to my father and my momma. After he said what he had to say, he went inside and closed the door behind him. The tears welled up in my eyes as the support system of my life was shattered in an instant. My momma said she loved me, but I couldn't tell, and my father had rejected me. We had been so close. He used to take me to my girl scout's meetings. He told me I was smart and that I would go to college. After all the love we had shared, his rejection now was the worst feeling in the world. I needed my father, but he made it perfectly clear that he would no longer support me. I was left feeling worthless, instantly stripped of the security that my earthly father provided.

Despite the lack of support I received from my family, what would take place the next morning would reveal the grace of God in my life once again and would give me something to hold on to. My momma and I went to see the principal of my high school. He looked at me very strangely. I just knew it was because I was beginning to show.

"Carmen, please have a seat with your momma," he said.

I slowly walked to the chair to sit down. I was so embarrassed. I could only imagine what he was thinking.

"Carmen, it appears that you've gained a little weight since the last time I've seen you?"

I looked around the room as if he weren't talking to me and did not respond to him. My momma quickly apologized for my behavior and corrected me at the same time.

"Mr. Jones, please forgive my daughter. It has come to our attention that Carmen is seven months pregnant. We have decided to move her to a home for unwed mothers and give the baby up for adoption. Therefore, she will not be returning back to school."

I was extremely disappointed, but again, I didn't say anything.

"Mrs. Washington, as you well know, Carmen's grades are exceptional and she is a model student. I would hate for her to miss out on the opportunity to graduate. I would like her to return to high school after she has the baby. That is, if it's okay with you."

"Yes, Mr. Jones, that's fine. Carmen?"

Instantly, I became very interested in the conversation and was so excited that I didn't know what to say.

"Yes, Momma," I answered with more hope in my heart than I'd felt in what seemed like an eternity. "I would love to come back."

"That's good. I'll see you after the baby is born," the principal said.

I knew God had heard my prayer. I was so happy that I would be able to complete my high school years at the same school.

The next day, my mom and I started searching for a home for unwed mothers. Day after day we continued to search, only to find there weren't any vacancies. I would have to stay at my parent's house after all. My father was not happy about it, but there was nowhere else for me to go. A couple months passed and I couldn't hide my pregnancy any longer. The neighbors started to gossip about my family. I felt so bad, but there was nothing I could do about it. I was the girl with a bad reputation — a verdict I didn't even deserve; but that didn't matter to people who had nothing better to do. They just continued to gossip and spread their lies until even my little sister was affected by it.

One day, she came home from school crying.

"What's wrong, Trease?" I asked.

"I don't want to talk about it!" she wailed, turning away from me.

"Trease, you were there for me when I needed you. Now tell me, what is it?"

"Okay," she sniffled, turning around to face me. "It's because of you that I'm crying."

"What do you mean, because of me?"

"Some boy came up to me after school and tried to . . ."

"Tried to what?" I demanded, afraid of what I was about to hear.

"He pushed me up against the wall and tried to take my pants down. He told me to give it up like you did and to stop being such a tease; so I bit him. Then he twisted my arm behind my back and I couldn't move. He tried to unzip his pants; so I raised my knee against him as hard as I could and he fell. I ran all the way home and I didn't look back. Why did he do that to me? Why?"

The thought ran through my mind, "I wish I was as strong as my little sister." I was so upset, but all I could do was hold her while she cried.

"Trease, I'm so sorry that happened to you. Please forgive me. I prayed that you would never have to face something like that."

I always carried the offenses of others upon my own shoulders as if they were my own fault. And now, I felt horrible about what happened to my sister because of the public shame of my pregnancy. I was powerless also to do anything about what happened to Trease, and my brother didn't make it any easier on me either. He had a song that he would sing by Little Richard called *"Annie Had a Baby and Can't Work No More."* He constantly teased me about being pregnant. I don't know why he wouldn't just leave me alone.

I tried to hide myself from my brother as well as from the neighbors, but it backfired on me that Christmas Eve while I was babysitting. I began to have horrible pains that I had never experienced before. At first, I took some aspirin, and then anything else I could find in the medicine cabinet. I felt like I was having a bowel movement, but I wasn't. Water ran down my legs. I could barely stand because of the terrible pain in my back, legs, and stomach. The pain got so intense that after a while I could no longer stand, so I laid on the floor. I didn't know what was happening to me. I cried out for help. It seemed like no one could hear me except the kids I was babysitting. They were just as afraid as I was, so they ran for help. Finally, I heard a knock at the door. I tried to get up and move toward it, but I couldn't. Then I saw one of the neighbors looking through the windows at me. The next thing I knew, my momma and father arrived at the house. My father picked me up and took me to Kaiser Hospital in Oakland, and my daughter was born that night.

SHOCK

Shock can be defined as a *sudden upsetting or surprising event or experience.* More seriously, it can be *an acute medical condition associated with a fall in blood pressure...caused by sudden emotional stress.* Carmen's entire young life had been one full of shocking and damaging experiences. Her mind, body, and emotions were never given the chance to recover before the next shocking blow occurred. The continual trauma combined with the forbidden ability to talk to anyone about any of it, left her in a state of mental, physical, and emotional turmoil that no one could understand. The turmoil left her spiritually confused, so there was no resting place, no seen door of escape. It is only a miracle of God that she survived, and a greater miracle still that she was later able to overcome and thrive as a result of it and lead countless others through to their place of victory also.

It is inevitable that we will all experience shocking moments in our lives that will seek to distract, detain, derail, and even destroy our purpose. This is why a deep prayer communion with the Father and a strong devotional life in His

Word are absolutely necessary in our daily lives. They will cushion us from the impact of the blows of life, and actually bounce or catapult us to greater heights in life.

I am a living witness of what God can and will do with a surrendered life. When the shocks of life leave you feeling as if there is no resting place, rest your head in the Word of God. He will minister His strength to you there and give you the direction to navigate through the trauma to the side of peace and victory.

When the storm has swept by, the wicked are gone, but the righteous stand firm forever. Proverbs 10:25 – (NIV)

Chapter Nine

GOD'S GIFT

"Momma...Momma...it hurts!"

"I know, but you've got to push."

"But it hurt's too much. I can't. Why does it have to hurt this much?"

"It'll be over soon, Carmen. Now push!" she ordered.

All I could think about was what Jason did to me and how! I never told anyone who he was out of fear. Our families were neighbors and friends. I believed they would say I was just blaming Jason and I was the promiscuous one. But who could blame them? I didn't even know I was pregnant until I was seven months along. My mind was not on pushing, but that didn't change anything. It was time to deliver.

"You have to push or the baby won't make it," my mom said.

I pushed with everything I had.

"I can't take it. It hurts too much," I insisted.

Then suddenly, there was silence.

"Here she is, Carmen, your beautiful baby girl!" the doctor exclaimed.

I saw her silky black, curly hair and chocolate brown skin; but she was quiet which drew concern that something was wrong.

"Why isn't she crying? What's wrong with her?" I asked, worried that I'd done something wrong.

"Nothing is wrong, Carmen. She just needs a little help breathing. I'll bring her back to you in a few minutes," the nurse said.

"Momma, where is she taking her? Why did she take her away?" I was beside myself, so my momma tried to calm me.

"Carmen, remember what we talked about? You agreed to give the baby up for adoption. When the nurse comes back, the social worker and adoption lady will be with her. Then it will be time for you to sign the papers. That will be the last time you see your baby. Do you understand what I am saying?"

I said nothing because I felt helpless. My momma shook her head and walked out of the room. I had a flashback to when I first got pregnant and how all this happened. It seemed like such a long time ago. But as I lay in the bed, the memories kept flooding back to how I didn't even know about how women became pregnant. How could I possibly not know that I was pregnant?

To this day, I can still remember the pain of childbirth while I was standing in bed at the hospital, contemplating jumping out the window. Thankfully, the nurse caught me, and my momma coached me through the rest of it. "Push, Carmen, push!" I will never forget the support of my momma during that painful time.

****

The day after my beautiful daughter was born, my momma, the social worker, and the nurse came back into my room and started making plans on what to do next. I looked over at my baby once again. Suddenly, God opened my mouth. I spoke out and I'm sure it shocked my momma.

"I . . . want . . . my . . . baby . . .!"

I scared myself when I heard my voice, and there was complete silence in the room. After a while my momma said, "If Carmen wants to keep her baby, I will not force her to give the baby up," she said to the social worker. The lady from the adoption agency left the room.

"Carmen, if you want to keep the baby, she will be your responsibility," momma said.

"I understand, Momma."

"I will find a caring person to take care of her during the day while you're in school, but you'll have to pick her up and drop her off at day care every day on time."

"Okay, Momma, I will. I'll take very good care of her," I promised.

"Are you sure you want to keep her?"

"Yes, I'm sure," I answered without a doubt in the world, rocking my baby in my arms and kissing her soft little cheeks. I thought to myself, "She's beautiful, not like me. I'll make sure no one ever hurts her." Then I looked into my precious daughter's eyes.

"Your name shall be, Marilyn." I talked to her out loud when we were alone. I knew she did not understand, but she was safe in my arms. "Oh sweetie, mommy's name is Carmen," I told her, as the memories from my school yard days when the boys teased me came flooding back. I remembered how the girls would ignore me and how much it hurt. It all came rushing back, and I could feel how their words still affected me even now. It didn't help that my mom reinforced some of those damaging ideas I was forming about myself with statements that I didn't understand.

Yet and still, regardless of the past, regardless of the circumstances surrounding my beautiful daughter's entrance into the world, and regardless of the fact that I knew absolutely nothing about being a mother, I knew in that moment that I was holding God's precious and tender gift to me in my arms.

PUSH!

Because of the lack of communication that continued in Carmen's home even into her pregnancy, she could not in any way imagine and was not prepared for the pain of childbirth. The combined fear and unbearable pain made her want to jump out the window.

Have the excruciating pains of life combined with the fear of uncertainty and the unknown made you want to 'jump out of a window'? It is at that very place that God is trying to birth something beautiful through you. The plans had all been made and settled for Carmen. She was to give the creation of God she had carried inside for nine months up for adoption. During the birthing process, all she could think about was the pain. But then, the moment she saw her beautiful daughter, all the pain, fear, regret, and uncertainty was instantly washed away by the joy of life she held in her arms.

It is time to forget the pain and the circumstances that brought it and focus on what God is trying to get *through* you. There is a gift in you that only *you* can give to the world. Don't give up on the delivery table and abort the gift! First identify what you are carrying and then *push* the beautiful thing out!

A woman giving birth to a child has pain because her time has come; but when her baby is born she forgets the anguish because of her joy that a child is born into the world. John 16:21 – (NIV)

****

As Marilyn grew, she had a special relationship with her momma. She was conceived through a selfish act, but from the moment Carmen held her beautiful daughter in her arms, she loved her just as God loved his Son, Jesus Christ. Suddenly, Carmen was holding in her arms a reflection of herself—a perfect little bundle of joy, ready to love and be loved, and completely untainted by the wickedness of others. Marilyn's birth represented Carmen's first restoration to purpose, so she could not help but love and want her. Because of the violation done to Carmen that caused Marilyn to be conceived, it was all-important to Carmen that she continually re-enforce to Marilyn her beauty and worth as a specially created gift from God.

Quite often ignorance and the lack of knowledge of who we are to God will cause us to not like the image we see in the mirror. If we are born from unpleasant circumstances, the problem is compounded. However, we must know that God never makes mistakes. People make mistakes, but God is the Master Craftsman who can transform the biggest of mistakes into the most wonderful gifts of God to the world. You are not an accident. You are full of undiscovered purpose. Learn to find your identity in the Word of God and not in the acts or manipulations of man.

Before I formed you in the womb I knew [and] approved of you [as My chosen instrument], and before you were born, I separated and set you apart, consecrating you; [and] I appointed you as a prophet to the nations. Jeremiah 1:5 - (AMP)

Chapter Ten

I DREAM ABOUT YOU

My mom came into the room while I was folding some laundry one day.

"Carmen, I'm going to pray that God will send you a husband, but not just any husband. I'm going to pray that God will send you a sailor. Sailors aren't too picky, and you need to get married because you have a child now."

I thought that I was so ugly that my mom had to pray for someone to marry me. I already felt unworthy and ashamed because of how my uncle treated me, but now even my own mom was confirming the worst about me. I was sure it showed on my face exactly how I felt about myself. Sometimes I felt as though people could see right through me.

"Carmen, did you hear what I said? I'm going to pray that God will send you a sailor for a husband."

"Yes, Momma, I heard you."

"Good, because God is going to send you a sailor. You just wait and see," she smiled and headed into the kitchen. "I'll see you when you get back from school. Make sure you pick up Marilyn on time."

"Okay, Momma, I will."

I was up late the night before studying for an exam, so I was exhausted. I got to school on time, but I had to stay after to make up some work. I hadn't communicated that to my mom, so when I got home late she was livid because she had to pick up Marilyn from daycare. She lit into me and made me feel like two-cents. She told me that she wasn't going to pay for daycare anymore. I did not tell her what happened. I cried all night because she tore my dream apart in a matter of minutes. My heart was broken. I had to drop out of high school. I enrolled in night school to get my high school diploma. I took care of my daughter during the day. I worked all day and stayed up most of the night. I was so tired that I barely had time to study, but I knew the Lord would take care of us. It soon became increasingly more difficult to do both.

Eventually, I was so exhausted that I dropped out of school and came home early one night. When I got home, Gary was in the kitchen with our mom to condemn me as usual.

"What are you doing home so early? Shouldn't you be in school?"

"I'm too tired. I can't do both," I said, sitting down exhausted.

"Uhm...that's what you get for getting pregnant. When my friend, Langston, comes over here tonight, don't you even think about going near him!"

Gary made me so angry. I was already feeling depressed about putting my dreams on hold, but his condemning words made me feel that much worse. I couldn't take too much more from him, nor his so-called friends. Regardless of how upset he made me, I still said nothing. I left the room. As I began to climb the stairs, I heard footsteps at the door and glanced toward it and back at Gary.

He looked at me like he wanted to slap me then and there.

"That's him. Let him in!" he ordered.

"Hello, how are you doing?" his friend Langston smiled.

"I'm fine, thank you," I softly replied.

"Carmen, what did I just say to you!" he yelled.

"Gary, I can hear you in the kitchen. Hush your mouth!" my momma said.

"But Momma, Carmen is up to her old tricks again. I told her to stay clear," Gary whined.

My momma came out of the kitchen and corrected him right in front of his friend.

"Gary, I raised you better than that. What's wrong with you, boy? If you don't show your sister some respect, you're going to regret it."

Gary was so ashamed because his new friend was standing right there.

"Now say you are sorry to your sister," momma ordered. Gary looked at her as if she was crazy. "I said say you are sorry to your sister."

"I'm sorry," he said reluctantly.

"Excuse me! I didn't hear you, and if I didn't hear you, neither did Carmen."

"I said I'm sorry, Carmen!"

"Gary, in the future, show some respect for your guest, as well as your sister," momma said with finality.

Gary dropped his head in shame, and I laughed on the inside because I felt he got what he deserved. Most families have some form of sibling rivalry, and ours was no different. Gary did not know that his friend Jason had raped me. If he had known, he probably would have been more of a protector, and our relationship probably would have been stronger. Momma went to the door to receive Gary's new friend.

"Hello Langston. It's nice to meet you. Welcome to our home," momma smiled.

"Thank you, Mrs. Washington. It's a pleasure to meet you."

"You have to excuse my son. He can be a bit overbearing at times, but I'm sure you know that."

"Yes, ma'am. No problem."

"So, how long have you known Gary?"

While my mom was talking to Langston, Gary was rolling his eyes at me, biting his lip, and shaking his head like he was about to burst into a million little pieces.

"I've known him for about three months now. We have class together."

"Oh, that's nice. Maybe you can get him to pay attention to his studies a bit more. He seems to be easily distracted by other people's affairs," she turned and looked at him.

"I'd be glad too, ma'am."

"Okay Carmen, let's go get dinner ready," my mom said. I started walking back into the kitchen with her, relieved somewhat that she came to my rescue when Gary attacked me verbally.

Langston called out, "It was nice to meet you both. Have a nice evening."

My mom replied, "We sure will, son. You're welcome to stay for dinner if you're still here when everything is ready."

"I'd be glad to, ma'am, but I'll only be here for about thirty minutes because I have something planned later."

"Okay, you're welcome to come to dinner anytime."

"Thank you for the invitation. I'll remember that." He turned to Gary and they went upstairs. I was relieved once again to see Gary leave the room and started helping my mom with dinner.

"Carmen, Langston is a respectful young man. I'm sure he'll be good for your brother."

"Maybe." I shrugged my shoulder because I just didn't care.

"I know that you're upset with your brother, but everybody makes mistakes, including him. He thinks he has it all together, but he still has a lot of growing up to do. He's still a boy, so be patient with him."

I looked at my daughter, took a deep breath, and collected myself.

"Just maybe, Langston can help your brother in the right direction. You never know. He might just be the one for you, too."

"Mom, what do you mean?"

"Oh, never mind. My prayer is that you marry a sailor, anyway."

Now I didn't know a lot about sailors. I only knew what I had heard, like they drank and cursed a lot and had a lot of girlfriends. Now my mom was once more planting in my mind that a sailor was the only person who would want me. But then again, that was the way my mom thought, and I never questioned her. I just took what she said at face value and never opened my mouth against her wishes. Getting married was not my desire. It was a demand she placed on me. When I look back now, I think she just wanted the best for me. She was only doing what her momma had taught her. I always thought she was strict. As time went on, I realized that she was only trying to protect me.

I found out a few years later just how much she cared. One beautiful summer day she was cooking in the kitchen. I was doing my household chores when I heard footsteps walking across the porch and a knock at the front door.

"Carmen, get the door, please," my mom called out. I went to the front door and looked out the peephole.

"Mom, I can't see who it is."

"Okay, don't open the door. I'll be there in a minute."

I waited for her to come to the door. She looked out the peephole, but she couldn't see either. She walked over to the living room window and slid the curtain back slightly. Then she turned around, looked at me, and smiled as she began walking toward the door, thanking God at the same time.

"Hallelujah! Praise the Lord! God has answered my prayer!"

I didn't know what she was talking about until she opened the door. It was Langston, but this time he was wearing a sailor suit! He looked so handsome in it. His eyes were extremely captivating as they changed colors in the light when he walked from outside to inside. His smile could easily melt a frozen stick of butter. Surely he wouldn't be interested in me, I thought to myself.

"Langston, you are an answer to prayer," my mom gushed.

"How is that, Mrs. Washington?"

My momma was looking at him like he was a piece of meat. I know that he must have felt awkward because I sure did.

"I don't quite understand," Langston smiled.

"Just come over here and sit down. Talk with Carmen while I go and get you two something cold to drink."

"Okay, Mrs. Washington."

As my mom exited the room, I sat uncomfortably, staring at random family photos.

"Excuse my momma," I said, apologizing on my mom's behalf. "She just likes sailors."

My mom came into the room again and put our drinks down.

"Here you go. I'll just be in the other room. It's good to see that you joined the navy, Langston. Take all the time you need."

She skipped out of the room singing. I was baffled. I didn't know what to think. I had never seen my mom act like that.

"Your mom likes sailors, huh? I guess that's a good thing for me," he laughed.

"I guess. Aren't you here to see my brother?"

"No, I didn't come over here to see Gary."

"So...why are you here?"

"I came to see you."

"Me?" I was surprised at his reply.

"Yes. I've wanted to ask you something for quite some time now."

"You have? And what is that?"

"Well, I'm not really the forward type, but you've been on my mind quite a bit lately. I think you're special."

I looked at him in disbelief. How could I be on his mind, and what in the world for? Surely this must be a joke Gary was trying to play on me; and using the word 'special' made me even more suspicious.

"You see, because I'm a sailor and travel a lot, I don't stay in one place very long. I haven't had a chance to really settle down."

"I don't really understand. What are you trying to say?"

Langston took a deep breath. "I guess I should just come out and say it. I haven't been able to sleep much lately and haven't been able to eat. When I do sleep, all I dream about is you."

"Did my brother put you up to this?"

"No, Carmen. It's not like that. Your brother doesn't even know I'm here."

"Then why *are* you here?"

"I was wondering if you would do me the honor of taking a walk with me someday?"

What? I thought to myself. I was taken aback. I got the feeling that with Langston, a walk meant so much more. He was perfect in my eyes, and gorgeous didn't even begin to describe him. I could only imagine where a walk with Langston would lead to. But if he tried anything, I'd call out to Jesus just like Trease did on my behalf!

"Yes, I will," I said, knowing this was my mother's prayer.

"I'm so glad you said yes! One day we'll take that walk. In the meantime, would you like to go to a movie with me on Saturday?"

"Okay, sure." I was sure my mom would approve. What was I supposed to say? My mom had already made it perfectly clear what she wanted.

"Great!" he said enthusiastically. He got up and walked toward the door.

"I'll see you on Saturday at 3:00 p.m."

"Okay. Bye, Langston," I smiled.

"Bye, Carmen."

I couldn't believe what just happened. I immediately called my mom because I knew she would be happy.

"Mom, guess what just happened?"

She quickly came running into the room flashing a big smile.

"Why are you smiling like that?"

"Because I know what you're about to tell me. The Lord just blessed in a mighty way."

"Mom, he just asked me to go to the movies with him on Saturday."

"You don't say."

"He also asked me to take a walk with him one day."

"Well child, I know what that means. Do you know what that means?"

"I'm not sure. Will you explain it to me?"

"Carmen, it means that God has provided you a husband."

"But Mom, why would God give me a husband?"

"Because He answers prayer. Come and sit down with me. Carmen, you're very special, but I know you don't think that you are. When you were born, I gave you a special name that means *joyful*. Somewhere along the line, your spirit was broken and you changed. I could see that you were hurting. That's why I prayed that God would send you a husband to love and accept you for who you are, to help bring the joy back into your heart and put a smile on your face."

I never realized that my mom was praying for me like that. I felt so blessed that she was my mom. However, I didn't want to be married. It was her desire so that I wouldn't be an unwed mother.

"Is that what Dad does for you, Mom?"

"Yes, Carmen, he does. A husband can put a smile on your face when there's nothing to smile about. He'll make your heart leap and put a skip in your step like nobody else can. A husband will provide for you and Marilyn so that you don't have to struggle."

As she continued speaking, I wondered if the reasons she spoke of were good reasons to get married.

"Trust me. The right husband is the best thing ever, and he will bring out the joy that's in your heart."

Is that what a husband is for? I thought to myself. "So, you're saying that I'll always be happy when I get married?"

"No. I'm not saying that. What I am saying is that when God blesses you with a husband, he'll take care of you; and he'll do his best to meet your needs. Just remember that he won't be perfect, but he will try to be for you. When he fails, be the woman he needs you to be."

"But Mom, I don't feel like a woman."

"You will baby. You will."

"When?"

"When Langston makes you feel like the most beautiful woman in the world. Then it will all make sense."

How could Langston make me feel beautiful? I thought to myself. Why did I even need a husband? All I wanted to do was go to school and get a degree in nursing at U.C. Berkeley, but my mom's mind was made up. I yielded to her voice as usual and submitted to her will by acting like I didn't know what she was talking about.

"How can he make me feel beautiful?"

"Carmen, you already are beautiful. Your baby Marilyn is a reflection of you."

WHOLENESS

Carmen was so much a part of Langston's heart that she was a part of his dreams, but she had a hard time believing that anyone would dream about her. She questioned his motives and doubted the truth of his words. He only wanted to love her, but she didn't believe she deserved his love, so she could not accept it.

Has there ever been a time when someone spoke kind words to you, but you couldn't accept them? Maybe you felt they wanted something from you when all they wanted was to show you they cared. Maybe their kindness triggered a negative memory within you that you could not explain. If this has happened to you, it's a sign that God wants to touch you and heal the broken pieces in your life.

Langston entered Carmen's' life to provide for her through a love relationship of closeness and transparency. Carmen often rejected Langston's expressions of love, but he continued to love her and provide for their family anyway. Langston's provision for Carmen re-ignited and released a desire within her to care for and protect those who are wounded and brokenhearted.

Although I did not know it then, my husband's unconditional love (which was a true reflection of our heavenly Father's love) was the catalyst that birthed the pastoral calling in my life. When you begin to accept the unconditional love of God, He will impregnate you with purpose beyond your imagination.

He heals the brokenhearted and binds up their wounds [curing their pains and their sorrows]. Psalms 147:3 - (AMP)

Chapter Eleven

JUST SAY THE WORD!

"Carmen. Carmen! Langston's at the door," my mom said.

"I'll be there in a second."

"Okay, I'll let him in for you."

"Thank you, Momma."

"No problem, baby," I heard her say as she opened the door.

"Hello, Mrs. Washington." I could hear them talking and laughing in the front room.

"Hello, Langston. It's a good thing you are so respectful. Many young men don't have good manners like you. Your parents raised you very well."

"Thank you, Mrs. Washington."

"You're quite welcome, son. Carmen will be ready in a few minutes. Would you like something to drink while you wait?"

"No, ma'am. I'm fine."

"Now don't be shy. I'll get you something to drink. I'll be right back. Have a seat. Carmen will be out in a minute."

As soon as my momma left for the kitchen, I walked out to greet Langston.

"Hello, Langston."

"Hello, Fair Lady. It's good to see you."

I chuckled at being called a fair lady. Then my momma came back into the room.

"Carmen, you look beautiful. Doesn't she, Langston?"

"Oh, yes ma'am. She most certainly does," he grinned.

"Where are you two going this afternoon?" she asked.

"Mrs. Washington, I'm taking her to the movies."

"That sounds nice. Now you two go along and have a good time."

"Okay, Mrs. Washington. We'll see you later," said Langston.

As we walked toward the door, he took my hand and opened the door for me, escorting me out.

"Now that's a gentleman," my momma chimed as we made our way down the stairs. "He's as gentle as all outdoors," we could hear her say.

I didn't understand what she meant, but I think Langston understood.

He replied, "Thank you, Mrs. Washington. We'll be back early."

"Okay. Enjoy the movie."

"Carmen, what movie would you like to see?"

"I don't really know what new movies are out."

"Don't worry because I have the perfect one in mind. I think you'll like it." "

"My favorite movie is Heidi. I saw it in school."

He smiled slightly. "But there's another one that I have in mind."

Langston opened the car door for me and off to the movies we went. All I could think about was, "Is this really happening?" As we approached the theater, I saw that he was taking me to see; "*Around the World in 80 Days*".

"I heard that this is a good movie. I told my sister that I wanted to see it," I said. I was so pleased to see what he had chosen.

"I know. She told me." he said with confidence. "That's why I picked it. I wanted to make sure that you would be happy because I love to see you smile."

"You talked to my sister about me?"

"I figured she would know you better than anybody else. You two are always together. So, as soon as I got the chance, I asked her what kind of movies you like, and she told me."

"What else did she tell you?"

"She didn't really say too much more. She just asked if I really liked you."

I couldn't believe Trease had asked him something like that, and I shook my head in disbelief.

"What did you say?"

"I told her, yes."

"I can't believe she didn't tell me. She normally tells me everything."

"I figured that, so I told her to keep it a secret."

"We don't keep secrets from each other."

"I know. She told me that too; but she said that since I really like you, she'd keep this one little secret."

"Why didn't you just ask me?"

"Because I didn't want to take any chances. You've been on my mind so much that I didn't want to blow it."

Even though he was looking right into my eyes and telling me how much he liked me, I still couldn't believe we were on a date.

"Why didn't you ask me and not someone else?"

"Carmen, because you've been heavily on my mind"

"Langston?"

"Yes, Carmen?" he answered.

"I think the movie is about to start."

"Oh, okay. I'll go buy the tickets."

He got out of the car and opened the door for me, and we went up to the ticket booth. I waited patiently while he purchased the tickets. He kept turning around, staring at me. I felt a little nervous, so I tried to avoid his eyes by aimlessly looking around. Once he purchased the tickets, we went inside.

"Carmen, would you like a soda and some popcorn?"

"Yes, thank you."

He reached into his pocket and pulled out his wallet and paid for our snacks.

"Good movie, Langston," the cashier said.

"Yes sir. I've heard about it through a very special person's sister."

"Would that special person be this beautiful young lady?"

"Yes, sir. Her name is Carmen."

"Well Carmen, it's good to see Langston with such a big smile on his face. He must really like you."

I was so embarrassed.

"Langston, she's absolutely lovely."

"Yes, I know," he smiled again.

I felt like someone was playing a trick on me because I really didn't think I was lovely at all. Langston sensed that I was a little uncomfortable because I was fidgeting with my hands and jacket, so he took my hand and we went inside the movie theater to sit down.

Once the movie finally started, I forgot about how uncomfortable the cashier made me feel. I was just glad that Langston worked up the nerve to ask me out, and I was happy just like my momma said I would be. Before I knew it, the movie was over and it was time to go back home. When we got to the house, Langston didn't want to leave just yet, so we sat on the porch for a little while.

"Thank you for taking me to the movie, Langston. I had fun."

"No problem, Sweets."

"Why are you calling me 'sweets'?" I laughed. "Because to me there's nothing sweeter than you, not even Sees® candy."

"How do you know?" I asked. "You don't even know me that well."

"I know that you're one of the sweetest girls around."

"How many girls do you know?"

"Enough to know that you're not like any of them, and I can't wait until we're married."

"Married? Don't you think that you're jumping the gun? You haven't even talked to my father yet."

"I'm not jumping the gun. I just wanted you to be the first to know that I plan on making you my wife."

"Why do you want to marry me? We haven't even known each other that long."

"Because I've always known you were the one for me."

"How could you know that?"

"Every time I see you, my heart skips a beat. Every time I hear you laugh, I smile inside. That's how I know. I don't feel like that about anybody but you. You are the one for me."

"But what if I don't feel the same way?"

"I love you enough for the both of us. You'll grow to love me someday."

I didn't know what to say, because no guy had ever talked to me that way. Then he took my hand, looked into my eyes, and whispered the words, "May I kiss you?"

I couldn't believe he asked me that. He was most definitely a gentleman. My momma was right. So, I gave him permission with a smile on my face. "Yes, you may."

Right before his lips touched mine, the screen door swung open and my father stepped out.

"What you kids doing out here?" my father yelled.

"We're just talking, Mr. Washington," Langston stepped back.

"Come on inside, so I can hear what you're talking about," he ordered.

We all went inside. I was much more nervous because I just knew my father was going to embarrass me.

"Langston, what are your intentions with my daughter?"

Oh my God! How could he do this to me? I thought to myself.

"Well, sir," he began.

Before Langston could get a word out, my father started talking again.

"Did you know she already has a little rug rat running around here? We don't want another illegitimate child popping up. I know how hormones work. I was young once too, you know. One minute you're smiling and the next minute you're kissing. Before you know it, you're pregnant! Ain't that right, Carmen?"

Those were the first words he spoke to me since I came home from my aunt's house after learning I was pregnant. It had been an entire year! I just sat there looking stunned because I couldn't believe he actually spoke to me.

"Carmen!" he repeated.

"Yes?"

"Yes what?"

"Yes, sir."

"That's more like it."

Langston could tell that I was hurt by what my father said, so he chimed in to take the pressure off me.

"Mr. Washington, I have every intention of marrying Carmen--with your blessing of course."

"Is that right?"

"Yes, sir. I'm a sailor, and I have a reasonable income. I can take care of Carmen and Marilyn."

"You sound like you've got this all worked out."

"No disrespect, sir, but I do. Carmen has a very special place in my heart, and all I want is for her to be happy," he persisted.

"Just remember after you marry her that I have already raised her. When you feel like you no longer want her, bring her home. Never raise your hand to her."

"Yes, sir. I would never do that. I just got a nice apartment and it's large enough for our new family. I would like to have your blessing. But with or without it, I plan on making Carmen my wife."

"Is that so?" he sneered.

"Mr. Washington, would you consider giving me your blessing to marry your daughter?"

My father lifted his foot up and firmly planted it on the floor and placed his chin in his hand when his elbow hit his knee. He cleared his throat and then threw his hands up. "Nobody else has asked her. So go ahead. Just don't expect me to pay for anything. And don't expect me to be there."

My father got up and walked out of the room. I tried to hold the tears back, but I couldn't. Langston put his arms around me to console me.

"Carmen don't cry. I'll take care of you, I promise. I love you, and I'll be a good husband. I'll take care of everything."

Within a matter of seconds my whole life transformed. Langston got on his knees, softly kissed my hand, and put a diamond ring on my finger.

PROVISION

Langston had a desire stronger than life to provide for Carmen. His heart was to take care of her and give her anything she wanted. She only needed to ask. However, she doubted his motives because her own damaging self-hatred caused her to doubt his genuineness. Carmen did not understand that Langston wanted to give her his best simply because he loved her.

Many of us—like Carmen--suffer through so many trials and tribulations that blind us. When God sends someone like Langston to be a gift to our lives, we can't see or appreciate what God has done to help us heal.

Carmen's mother wanted her to marry a sailor because she believed that the United States military recruited young men who were healthy, mentally sound, and practiced good Christian moral values. She also believed that a military man would have a sound enough income to sufficiently support a wife and family. When Langston came along, Carmen knew that her mother's prayers had been answered. Langston was a Christian and was very handsome, respectful, gentle, and generous. Langston was the husband for Carmen, but she was not ready to receive him or to be his wife.

Carmen had not resolved or released her mind and body from the long past sexual abuse by her uncle. She had not forgiven her father or released the rejection she had received from him after Marilyn was born. Once Carmen came to understand that she had to forgive to be free and release her mind to benefit from what God had planned for her life, a shift for the better began to take place—even though she would not see the immediate manifestation of it for some time.

God has spoken many promises in His Word to us. Often, we doubt the promises of God because of the things we see and the obstacles we face. Sometimes we even believe that God's Word doesn't work for us, even though it works for everyone else. If we allow ourselves to believe this way, God's Word will remain stagnant in our lives. Therefore, we must make a conscious effort to align our thoughts and beliefs with the Word of God. When we believe and speak the Word, it will manifest itself in glorious ways in our lives.

For all the promises of God in him are yea, and in him Amen, unto the glory of God by us. 2 Corinthians 1:20 - (NKJ)

Chapter Twelve

EVERY INCH OF ME

"Carmen, hurry up and get your dress on. They're waiting for you in the church," Trease shouted.

"I'm going as fast as I can. I thought this was my day. Why is everybody rushing me? I don't know if I can do this. I really don't know if I can." I was panicking, even though I knew this was momma's wish. Then I turned around and looked at my sister.

"Trease, what am I doing? I'm not sure that I can do this. I'm just not sure. What if he's not the one? What if he's like...?" I stopped before finishing my sentence. I wasn't sure if I wanted to hear myself say the words out loud, and especially not to my little sister.

"Like whom, Carmen?" she asked.

I immediately flashed back to the days of the incestuous episodes that I tried so hard to block out of my memory. I heard my uncle's voice, just as if he was standing in the room with me. I froze. *You gone be so happy. Happy you'll be. No other niece, as special to me. You gone be so happy. Happy you'll be. Remember, not to move, because you'll spoil the surprise.* When I snapped back to reality, I felt empty inside, and I freaked out! I could feel my heart beating through my chest like it was about to explode.

"Oh my God, I can't go through with this!"

"Sis, you've just got butterflies. You're going to be just fine. Take a deep breath and let it out. Langston loves you. He'll take very good care of you. Don't worry so much. Now turn around so I can button your dress."

"Okay, okay. Let me pull myself together."

I inhaled and then I exhaled, looking at myself in the mirror. I took another deep breath, turned around, and released a sigh of relief when I looked into my sister's eyes. She helped me finish getting ready.

"Trease, I love you so much. What would I do without you? You've always been there for me."

"I know, and I always will. I love you Big Sis."

"I love you too, Little Sis."

The music began to play, and it was time to take that walk. I was scared for my life because I knew what would happen after I became Langston Alexander's wife. Trease kissed me on the cheek and then walked out the door. I looked in the mirror at myself once again. The dress I had on reminded me of the dress my uncle gave me when I was just seven years old. I knew it was just a matter of time before it had to come off. I closed my eyes and tried to forget the memory of my uncle's touch, but it didn't work. All of a sudden, I became very cold and tears formed in my eyes. I tried to shake myself out of it. I fluffed my hair and walked out the door toward the entryway. To my surprise, my father was there waiting for me with a box of tissues in hand.

"You look like a vision, Carmen. You're absolutely beautiful. Now stop crying. Everything is going to be just fine."

"I can't believe you came. What made you change your mind?"

"Langston looked me in my eyes and told me that he was going to marry you, with or without my blessing. I didn't want to miss your special day."

There was that word again. He kissed me on the forehead and proceeded to walk me down the aisle. I was so happy that my father approved of my marriage, and that I was no longer an embarrassment to him. I linked my arm in his and took a deep breath. The two of us walked down the aisle together. When the preacher asked, "Who gives this woman in marriage?" my father proudly said, "I do."

Langston took my hand and began reading his vows to me. "Carmen, I love you. I will take care of you for the rest of my life. Every inch of me needs you, and I will cherish you from sunrise to sunset. You are the good thing that God has given me. *For he that findeth a wife, findeth a good thing and obtains favor of the Lord.* Because of you, Carmen, I am now complete in you and in Christ. I thank God that you said yes to be my wife. Today, I give you my love, my heart, my dreams, and my passions. You are the keeper and the protector of my heart. Sweets, today I freely give you every part of me."

I almost laughed out loud because he looked so serious standing in front of me like he was saluting his sergeant. Then he put a beautiful wedding band on my finger. I could hardly hold back my tears when it was time for me to open my heart to him with words I had never spoken to any man.

"Langston, I thank you for giving your heart to me and choosing me as your wife. I promise to care for you, in sickness and in health. I promise today..." I could barely say another word, so I whispered in his ear. "I like you." I placed his wedding band on his finger. The preacher asked, "Do you take this woman to be your lawfully wedded wife?"

"I do," Langston beamed.

"Do you take this man to be your lawfully wedded husband?"

I looked at Langston and saw the love in his eyes. "Y-e-s-s-s-s, I do." I just wasn't sure I could do this.

"By the powers vested in me, by the State of California, and the city of Berkeley, I now pronounce you husband and wife. Langston, you may now kiss your bride."

Langston leaned over, touched my chin, and kissed me.

"Ladies and gentlemen, I present to you, Mr. and Mrs. Langston Alexander."

Everyone stood up and started clapping and cheering. They watched us walk down the aisle together as husband and wife. There wasn't a dry eye in the church. Everyone joined in, singing, and laughing as the music played. Langston took my hands and swirling me around to the music, pulled me close to him and started singing to me. To my surprise, Langston had an amazing golden voice, but I still felt very uncomfortable because I knew it was almost time for him to take my garter off. As he continued to sing to me, I became even more nervous and began fidgeting. Suddenly the wedding coordinator called out, "Langston, it's time to take the garter off," she said with a loud voice.

"Alright, let the honeymoon begin," he happily shouted out. "Okay, Sweets, let's get started."

I thought to myself, Oh my God...rolling my eyes at the thought of him touching my thigh. I slowly sat down in the chair my sister decorated for me. Langston swiftly lifted my dress to take the garter off my leg. I felt myself getting angry as he slid the garter off my thigh with his teeth. Instead of objecting or telling him how I felt, I kept smiling, while feeling violated at the same time. I realized that I was his wife now, and I had a duty to perform. But would I be able to? I thought to myself. Once he had the garter off, I quickly jumped up like the roof was on fire!

"It's time to throw the bouquet. Everybody line up," I said as I motioned for everyone to gather together. I turned around and closed my eyes, then threw the bouquet over my shoulders. When I opened my eyes and turned around, Langston was licking the chocolate off his fingers from our cake, beckoning me over to him and walking toward me. I took one step toward him. I froze in fear, thinking that he deserved better. I looked at Trease and my daughter standing together.

"Don't worry about Marilyn. I will take care of her while you are on your honeymoon." Trease said. "Marilyn, are you ready to have some fun?"

"Yes, auntie, I am."

Langston looked lovingly into my eyes, smiled, and took my hand. "Carmen, it's time to leave," he whispered as he kissed my cheek.

I thought to myself, he sure likes to kiss. "Okay. I just need to do one more thing," I said, trying to delay fulfilling my obligations without being too obvious.

"C'mon, Sweets, let's go now. I can't wait any longer."

I finally submitted to his voice, and we immediately left the reception. When it was time for the honeymoon to start, I decided to stay in the bathroom for as long as I possibly could. Eventually Langston got impatient.

"Sweets, what are you doing in there? You've been in the bathroom for an hour. This is our wedding night. Come out of there or I'm coming in to get you!" he laughed.

"I'm coming. I'll be out in a minute. I'm just changing into something nice for you. I want everything to be just perfect."

"Yeah, that's what I'm talking about. Get it ready for papa."

I heard him humming to himself. I peeked out the bathroom door. He was fixing the sheets and fluffing the pillows. I came out of the bathroom with sweats on, my hair rolled up, and cream on my face.

"Carmen, you do realize that this is our wedding night, right?"

"Yes, I do."

"Then why in the world are you dressed like that? What happened to your beautiful hairstyle? And what's with all that cream on your face? Why are you wearing sweats? Papa can't work with that."

"I thought you said you loved every inch of me?"

"Sweets, I can't even see you!"

"What do you mean, you can't see me? I'm right here."

"I don't mean that. I mean...I don't know what I mean," he sighed with frustration.

"Well, I'm going to sleep," I said quickly, hoping he would let me slip into bed and that would be that —for tonight anyway.

"Carmen, baby, don't be like that. I didn't mean anything by it. I just want tonight to be special. I promise I won't hurt you. I'll be gentle. It's our first night together, and I need to be with you. I really need to be with you tonight."

The word special sent shock waves to every part of my body. I just couldn't get past my past and rejected his husbandly advances.

"We'll have more nights," I softly said, trembling. I took a deep breath and lay completely still. I knew that I would have to be his wife soon, but tonight was not that night.

LOVE

Carmen couldn't fathom that someone would cherish her to the point that every part of him would belong to her. She was still stuck in the past, feeling inadequate. Langston was intent on showing her how much he loved her through his words and deeds. Yet, Carmen would still hold herself back because she was unfamiliar with that kind of love.

The love of man only goes so deep, but God's love is unconditional, and it is so deep that it is unfathomable to the human mind. If you are a parent, can you imagine giving your child up to save another person's child? Yet, that is exactly what God did for us. He loved us so much that He gave us His very best in the form of His Son, Jesus Christ to save us.

Consequently, Carmen did not perish because God sent her a loving, nurturing, provider as a husband, and an excellent father to their children. Langston also provided the means for Carmen to start releasing old memories that would in turn began the process of healing her mind.

Accept the love of Christ and let it wash away all of the dross of your past. Allow God to process the diamond that you are so that His light of deliverance can be released to the world through you.

For God so greatly loved and dearly prized the world that He [even] gave up His only begotten (unique) Son, so that whoever believes in (trusts in, clings to, relies on) Him shall not perish (come to destruction, be lost) but have eternal (everlasting) life. John 3:16 - (AMP)

Chapter Thirteen

THREE BARS OF SOAP

Six months went by and we still hadn't consummated our marriage. Langston was growing extremely frustrated with me. Yet, he was still as patient as he could be. I knew I wasn't making it any easier on him because I had a thing about looking good everywhere I went — everywhere except for the bedroom. He would make comments that I was dressing up for everybody but him; and I was wrongly thinking that I rather him get someone else to meet his physical needs than to wait for me, but I didn't dare tell him that. However, I knew it would be just a matter of time before my rejection of him would soon bear its fruit.

One morning he came home around midnight. When he got into bed I thought I smelled a woman's perfume.

"Where have you been?" I asked.

"I was just out with the boys," he said with frustration in his voice.

"Out with the boys?" I persisted.

"Yeah, you know sometimes we just like to sit around and talk about guy things."

"Until midnight? Don't you think that's kind of late?"

"We lost track of the time."

"Langston, I miss you when you're not here."

"I'm here now, and you don't have to miss me or feel bad about not consummating our marriage."

I cuddled up alongside him, but he turned his back to me. Even though he said I didn't have to feel bad, I did. I knew that my rejection of him had taken its toll. I just didn't realize how much.

"Carmen, there's something I need to tell you."

He suddenly turned around and looked me in the eyes. I didn't know what to think because he had a very concerned look on his face.

"What is it?" fearing what he might say.

"I have to go out to sea for six months. I've been called to duty."

"When did you get called?" I asked, surprised by the news.

"They called me today."

"Today?" I gasped. "Why didn't you come home sooner and tell me?"

"I don't feel that you like or even want me. So I have to deal with it in my own way and in my own time."

"Langston, I do like you." I said honestly.

"When you like someone, Carmen, you don't treat them the way you have treated me. I feel like you don't want or need me, nor have my needs been met. When I needed you--really needed you--you rejected me on our wedding night...of all nights."

"Langston, I'm so sorry," feeling just terrible for rejecting him.

"It's too late to be sorry. You ruined the most important night of our lives. And now, I'm going to be gone for a very long time. I don't even know when or if I'll be back--or if I even want to come back. I've tried to be patient. But now, I'm just tired of waiting. Do you think it's fair that you've made me wait this long? I'm your husband for God's sake!"

"I don't know what to say," I stammered.

"You sure don't. And you sure as hell don't know what to do. I'm going to sleep."

He punched his pillow into shape and turned away again.

"Langston, please don't be like that."

"Like what?" he asked, rolling around to face me. "You expect me to take care of you and be there for you, but you don't reciprocate it. How patient do you expect me to be? I need you to be my wife in every sense of the word, from the crown of your head to the soles of your feet. Remember our wedding vows? Were you just saying words that you didn't even mean?"

"No, I said I liked you." I was not emotionally ready for marriage, and I knew he was angry with me. I had to do something quick. What would my momma say if he left me? So I placed my lips on his and whispered, "I'm ready now."

He hesitated, "Are you sure?"

"Yes, I'm sure."

We came together as one for the first time. I truly felt different, just not like my momma said I would. The way he touched me was nothing like Jason's or my uncle's touch. It was different. The next morning it was time for him to leave, so I prepared his things for his departure. He watched while I began packing his bags. The whole time he kept staring at me, as if he had something on his mind.

"Carmen, you know that I love you, don't you?"

"Yes, of course I do. But I am wondering why you've been staring at me like that."

"Because you are the most beautiful woman I've ever seen. That's why it hurts for me to tell you this."

"Tell me what? What are you talking about?"

"I've always had a hard time dealing with rejection. When you rejected me, well I..." he stopped.

"You what? What did you do?"

"I'm not proud of what I did, but I need for you to forgive me."

"Forgive you for what?" I asked, a little scared.

"Well, like I said," he started again, "I've always had a hard time dealing with rejection. I was approached by a woman last night."

"Last night, when?" startled at what he was saying.

"Right before I came home. Before I came home to you last night, I was with another woman." I couldn't believe what he was telling me. "All the time we've been together, you've kept rejecting me."

"I wasn't rejecting you. I didn't know how to be with you," I cried.

"What was I supposed to think? You wouldn't talk to me about it. Every time I tried to be with you, you just pushed me away."

"I was afraid, Langston."

"Afraid? You didn't have to be afraid of me. I just wanted and needed to be with you, but you wouldn't let me."

"Do you like her?"

"No, I don't, but she was just someone waiting in the wings to comfort me."

"Waiting in the wings? Were you planning on this from the start just in case it didn't work out?"

"Not really. It just happened. I needed to feel loved."

"You needed to feel loved? Sex is not love, or don't you know the difference?"

"I needed you. When I was with her, I called out your name. Carmen, I am so sorry. Please forgive me. I love you so much. I made a huge mistake, and I need you to forgive me. I need you to forgive me before I leave."

He started to cry, and I couldn't help but forgive him. Besides, I felt like it was my fault for turning him away repeatedly. Outwardly, I told him I forgave him, but inwardly I hadn't. I'm sure he could sense that I was still upset with him.

"Ok, let's just finish packing, so you can leave!" I retorted.

He kept apologizing and telling me how much he loved me, but we both knew the damage had already been done.

"You can take this black bag and I'll take the tan ones," he said.

"Okay, I have it."

We walked toward the car to put his bags into the trunk. Langston opened the trunk, turned around, and looked at me with sorrow in his eyes. I knew then that he really did regret what he had done.

"Carmen, always remember that I love you and Marilyn. I love you both more than life itself." He kissed Marilyn on the cheek and hugged me like he would never return.

"I'll remember," I said, unforgivingly looking into his eyes.

"I'll be back." He wrestled to assure me, with doubt in his voice.

I watched my husband drive away, not knowing when or if he would ever come back; but I kept my composure, even though I felt I could never trust him again. I did not realize it at the time, but Langston pouring his heart out to me was exactly the one reason I did have to trust him. The unresolved issues of my childhood rejected the very thought that he could be honest with me. I still had to deal with the unresolved issues that made me feel filthy and utterly unclean after he touched me. I needed to thoroughly cleanse myself to get rid of the scent that attached itself to my skin. At that very moment, I made a plan in my mind for just how I would get clean, and I took Marilyn back into the house.

"I want you to sit here and play while I go to take a shower."

"Okay, Momma," she said, starting to play with her dolls.

I quickly undressed myself and got into the shower. I remember using three bars of soap and a Brillo pad. I scrubbed my entire body until the steel pad was beet red from the rawness of my skin. I realized the shame of my youth had resurfaced once again; but *this* time, I was determined to wash away every last issue.

LIFE

Carmen could not bear to look at herself in the mirror any longer. She wanted so badly to wash away the residue of the memories that were in her mind and the dirtiness of the hands she could still feel touching her. She felt that cleaning herself to the point of self-mutilation would somehow erase the filth she felt on the inside.

When the cares of life overwhelm us, we can form a habit of pushing ourselves to do more than is humanly possible in an attempt to drown out what is hurting us. We can wear ourselves out trying to erase the past, instead of embracing the lessons the past taught us. Yes, it is difficult to embrace all of the painful experiences that have happened to us. However, it is God's purpose and will for us to use the negative experiences in our lives to help others overcome similar circumstances. Without the personal journey of injury and healing God led me through, it would be impossible to help others find the road to recovery.

We are assured and know that [God being a partner in their labor] all things work together and are [fitting into a plan] for good to and for those who love God and are called according to [His] design and purpose. Romans 8:28 - (AMP)

Chapter Fourteen

SPIRITUAL AWAKENING

One Sunday morning I got up early because I wanted to go to church. When we first moved to the neighborhood I spotted a church not too far from the house. It was called Liberty Church. I was attracted to the name, so I wanted to visit. My heart was still hurting about how Langston and I had left each other when he departed for duty. I needed something to take my mind off my pain. I got myself together and made sure Marilyn had her Sunday best on. I still hadn't really learned how to be a mother, but I took great pains to make sure Marilyn was always dressed like a precious doll. She was my precious baby girl. I would often go to the thrift store and find cute second-hand clothes. I would take the clothes home, wash, and starch them until they looked brand new. No one ever knew my baby wore second-hand clothes.

When we arrived at church, the choir was already singing. *He'll wash away, He'll wash away the stains of my past--every one! He'll wash away, He'll wash away the shame of my youth. Yes, He will!* I just sat there as the choir sang, thinking about how I couldn't be a wife to my husband because of the memories from my childhood. All I wanted was for those memories to disappear and to be healed from the stains of my past. As the choir continued to sing, the words that I heard didn't register in my mind. I was lost in painful memories and didn't even hear the sermon. Before I knew it, service was already over.

"Hello sister, I haven't seen you around here before. Are you new in the neighborhood?" the pastor asked.

"Yes, Pastor. My name is Carmen. My husband, Langston, and I have lived here for about six months."

"Welcome to the neighborhood and to our church. Where is your husband now?"

"He was called to duty and just set sail yesterday morning. It's just me and our little girl, Marilyn." Marilyn was sitting on the pew, playing with her dolls.

"You've come to the right place. We'll take good care of you and your daughter. We'll also keep your husband lifted up in prayer."

"Thank you, Pastor."

"That's what we're here for. Come over here so you can meet some of the members of our church."

"Okay. Thank you, sir."

I smiled because of his hospitality. We walked over toward some of the members of the church, and he introduced me to them.

"Sister Carmen, these are the Pillars of Praise of Liberty Church--Maya, Bridget, Elyse and Keith."

"The Pillars of Praise?" I asked, surprised at their name.

"They're the praise and worship leaders of the church. Even though they're young, they know how to approach the throne of God. They are prayer warriors with praise in their hearts. Sister

Elyse is also the church secretary, and Keith is our musician."

"Nice to meet all of you," I smiled.

"Nice to meet you also," said Keith.

"Welcome to our church. It's nice to meet you," said Maya, Bridget, and Elyse.

"What are you doing after church?" asked Maya.

"I'm taking my daughter to the park. I can tell she's getting bored playing with her dolls," I said, glancing in her direction.

"What's your daughter's name?" Keith asked.

"Her name is Marilyn."

"She's beautiful just like her momma," he said under his breath.

"I don't really have any other plans," I replied.

"Nonsense. Come with us. We're going out to get something to eat at a really good restaurant a couple of blocks from here. They have the best vanilla milk shakes and french fries I've ever tasted." Maya insisted.

"Are you sure it's alright?"

"Sure it's okay," Bridget and Elyse agreed.

"No sense in sitting around on this lovely day," Bridget continued. "What about you Keith. Are you coming?"

"No, I'll see you all later. I have to practice for next Sunday's service."

"Okay! Let's go get something to eat," the ladies said.

We all left together, just us girls. It was a nice change, having girlfriends to talk to over lunch. Bridget told me that she was a prophet. She reminded me of myself because she didn't speak much, but I could tell she was very intuitive.

Elyse, however, was a whole different breed of a woman. She was very loud and was saying everything that came into her mind. I could tell that Maya was a prayer warrior because she never stopped praying from the time we left the church until the time we arrived at the restaurant. I finally got her attention.

"Maya, how long have you been attending Liberty Church?"

"I was raised in Liberty Church. My parents are both active members. We visit other churches, but there's no place like home. Ain't that right, Bridget?"

"She's not asking about me right now. She's asking about you," said Bridget.

Maya continued, "I've been at Liberty Church for over ten years. It's where I learned to pray. I love to pray everywhere I go, no matter what time of day or night. It's probably because all I know is church. Sometimes I don't know if that's good or bad. How about you, Bridget?" she asked.

"You insist that she knows about my fall away," Bridget fumed.

"What fall away?" I asked, glancing over at Marilyn, who was busy with the coloring book the waitress gave her.

"Since Maya keeps bringing it up, I'll tell you. About a year ago, I got a little antsy. I wanted to see what the world had to offer me, since I was also raised in the church 24-hours a day, seven days a week. God gives me things to say to people, and they come true. That's how I knew God had a call on my life, and I wanted to experiment. One day, I told a lady she was pregnant, and sure enough, she was. Another time, I told the same lady she was going to have a baby girl, and she did," Bridget said proudly.

"Were you scared to speak up?" I asked.

"At first I was. But then it became quite natural to me."

"Really? Then what happened?"

"I decided to step outside the box and dibble and dabble in the unknown. I just wanted to find out what was on the other side and all. I figured since sometimes I knew things in advance, if anything crazy was about to happen, I would be the first to know."

"So, what happened?" I asked Bridget with heightened interest.

"I got a rude awakening, that's what happened. I tried to use my gift for gain. I got an office and everything. People paid big money to see me. It's amazing what people will do for a little taste of the future. It was easy until I got whipped upside the head. God was not having any of it."

"What do you mean?" I asked.

"I was tormented. I was having nightmares. I kept feeling like something was in the room with me. My skin would crawl, and I had an uncontrollable itch. I couldn't sleep, and every time I tried to, I felt like something, or someone was gnawing on me. I was throwing up every day and was always sick to my stomach. My skin was turning all shades of pale. My real friends said I looked like death was calling my name. Funny thing is, that's exactly what I was dealing with," she took a deep breath. "Thank God for delivering me!"

"I always thought you were blowing that out of proportion," Elyse commented. "It wasn't that serious! A little white magic never hurt anybody, right? Sometimes, that's what it takes to get what you want."

"That's why you don't have a husband now," warned Maya.

"You got a sister twisted," Elyse corrected her. "I get what I want, and all it takes is a little white powder," she persisted.

"Baby powder has never gotten anybody a man," Maya said.

"I'm not talking about that kind of powder," Elyse sighed. "Anyway, I haven't found the right man yet."

"You do know what it says in the Bible about looking for a man, don't you?" Maya asked.

"Yeah, I know. But I'm a creative being. My white powder is the next best thing." Elyse took out a little transparent vile and started rolling it around in her right hand with her fingers. "This is one of my little creations. All I have to do is put it in a warm pot of water, let it come to a slow boil, and watch the powder rise to the top. Once it rises, it's ready to be used for the purpose I created it for. That's when I sprinkle a little in my bath water. Not too much, and not too little. The ingredients have to be just right."

"Just right for what?" I asked.

"Just right for me to soak in and saturate every inch of my fabulous skin; so when a brother wants to creep in, I'll be ready for him."

"That's wicked," Maya said.

"What you call wicked, I call smart. My creation has the power to deliver a man right to my front door and into my bed. So when Mr. Right comes knocking on my door, well, let's just say he'll be in for the whole night. His body may leave in the morning, but his mind will be mine."

I don't think any of us could believe what we were hearing. Then again, it didn't appear that Elyse bit her tongue about anything. It was obvious that she was used to doing things her own way and getting exactly what she wanted. I was glad that Marilyn had fallen asleep and hadn't heard anything she was saying.

"Don't get me wrong," Elyse continued. "I'm not desperate. It's got to be a fine brother, one that can lay down the law, Billie club and all."

"That's why you keep missing out, Elyse. You're too busy trying to help God out. He don't need your help," Maya preached.

"Maya, as you well know, I've been single for a long time, and my clock is ticking."

"You're taking way too many chances, trying to land a man the wrong way," Maya cautioned.

"I'm not trying to land one. I plan on springing one! And once he's sprung, I know how to keep him coming back. He'll be so sprung he won't know whether he's coming or going. All he'll be able to do is think about pleasing me!" Elyse laughed.

"Why would you go through all that?" I asked.

"Like I said, my clock is ticking. You got a husband. Do the math."

"God will send you a husband when you're ready. It has nothing to do with your clock," I said.

"Well, this little white powder is exactly what I need to speed up the minute-hand."

"It's gonna take more than that to keep a man," Maya argued.

"If he even thinks about leaving me, well, I got something for that too. The doctors can't even diagnose it," Elyse retorted.

"You need to stop playing with God," Maya cautioned.

"When I'm done with him, he'll think I am God," Elyse laughed again, but no one else thought it was very funny.

Maya chimed in, "That's why I had to pray Bridget through, because of sistas like you messing in things they shouldn't. You made her want to dibble and dabble around, and she got all messed up!"

"I plead the fifth. She did that on her own. I didn't have anything to do with that," Elyse objected.

"Yeah right. That's why she was walking around here with white lips and black circles under her eyes."

"How did I know she would try to copy me? I would have told her, you can't duplicate... perfection!"

"She looked like death on wheels. I had to labor for her in prayer for ten days straight," Maya insisted.

"We all know that you can get a prayer through! Thank you for sharing, Maya," Elyse ranted.

"I'm just saying, when you need a prayer warrior, just call me. I'll be there for you! I'll be there. You don't have to call 9-1-1, just call M-O-M-M-A, 'cause I got your back!"

We all laughed. Elyse started to get loud because our order hadn't been taken yet, waking up Marilyn in the process.

"Where is the waiter? I'm hungry! I don't know why we even come here. Every time we come to this restaurant we wait for hours for them to take our order. Hours, I'm telling you."

"Momma, I'm hungry," said Marilyn.

"So am I!" Elyse complained.

"We don't wait for hours. You're just hungry," Maya laughed.

"That's what I said. Ain't that what I said, Bridget?"

"Yes, Elyse. Here she comes now to take our order."

"Well, it's about time. I'm about to starve up in here."

"You are over-exaggerating. Calm down," Maya said.

"I am calm. I'm just hungry. I needs to feed my flesh, and a sista's got to eat. I need me some beef."

"May I take your order?" the waitress asked.

"Yes, I would like a steak—a T-bone steak. You know, a steak on a stick. And make sure you bring a lot of A1® steak sauce," she demanded.

"Yes, ma'am."

"Do I look like your momma? Just give me some mashed potatoes and freshly chopped green beans on the side," Elyse demanded.

"Okay, got it," the waitress smiled, trying not to make it obvious that Elyse was getting on her nerves.

"Oh yeah, make sure my beef is well-done, but not crispy."

"Okay," the waitress replied politely.

Maya ordered for the rest of us. "We'll all take the number five, please."

The waitress repeated the order and Maya confirmed it. "What about the little girl?"

"She'll be eating with me, thank you," I assured her.

"Okay, I'll be right back with your waters."

"Did I ask for water? I just want her to bring me my food," said Elyse.

"You need to lay off that beef. That's why you act so fleshly." Maya said turning to me. "You have to excuse her, Carmen. She doesn't know how to act."

"Oh, here we go again. The most 'holier than thou' hast blessed us with her most holy word," Elyse pouted, rolling her eyes. But then she turned back to address Maya, "Would you like to pray over the food sister--to make sure there are no pesticides, homicides, or genocides in the secret sauce?"

Maya took a deep breath, "Elyse, stop being so sarcastic. We have a guest with us. Show some dignity. You're going to scare her away and make her think that we all act like you."

"Oh, excuse me! Carmen, you have to understand. I haven't had a man in a while, and I needs to tame the beast, if you know what I'm saying," she winked.

"I guess so," I shrugged.

"See? She understands. Shoot, she got a baby. She didn't get that baby drinking water and jumping rope. She knows what it's like to have a man, don't you, Carmen?"

"I really don't want to talk about that," I said quickly, hoping she would just drop the subject altogether. I suddenly felt very uncomfortable. I turned toward Marilyn again to see how her coloring was coming along.

Maya addressed me, "Don't mind her, Carmen. Like she said, she's just hungry," she smiled. The next thing we all knew, Elyse was standing up screaming at the top of her lungs.

"Waiter, waitress, hostess, busboy, bellman — somebody bring me some beef!"

I sat there embarrassed because Elyse was so loud and drew so much attention to herself and to us. I started silently praying that God would bring her a husband with speed, because she needed one just to calm her flesh down. Right when I finished praying, a waiter came over to our table and offered his assistance.

"How can I help you, miss?"

"Well, we just placed our order with the waitress, but since you're here, there is something that you can help a sista out with," Elyse flirted.

"What is that, miss?"

"First, you can stop calling me 'miss'. My name is Elyse. Secondly, you got a phone number so we can talk in private?"

"I don't give out my number. It's against the restaurant policy."

"Well, I'll make it worth your while to break that policy."

I couldn't believe my ears. Elyse was over the top. But the waiter stunned all of us with his quick response to her.

"The fact is, miss, I like a soft-spoken woman of mystery and you're an open book." He turned away from her and looked at us. "Is there anything else I can help you ladies with?"

Before anyone of us could answer, Elyse made a lame attempt to engage him in conversation again. "Since you don't have a name badge on, can you tell us your name?"

"My name is Jeffrey."

"Never mind her, Jeffrey. Can you please bring us some sodas while we wait for our food?" Maya asked.

"I'll be glad to. What kind would you like?"

"I'd like a Coke," Maya said.

"Okay." He turned and looked at me. "What would you like to drink, miss?"

"Coke is fine for me, also."

"What about you two ladies?" he asked, addressing Elyse and Bridget.

"We'll both have Cokes," said Bridget.

"Ah, the prophet speaks once again. How does she know so much?" Elyse said sarcastically.

"You need to stop playing," warned Maya.

"Girl, I'm just kidding. Cokes will be just fine." Jeffrey walked away to get our drinks.

Elyse almost fell off her seat watching him.

"Girl, if that ain't a little piece of heaven in them there Levi's, I don't know what is. Then again, I know exactly what's in them jeans," she giggled, then raised her head to the heavens speaking in the air. "Deliver him to me, oh Lord. Send Maya 9-1-1! Make haste and deliver that brotha to me."

"Elyse! Get a hold of yourself," Maya ordered.

"I am. That's the problem."

Jeffrey came back to the table with our drinks and started placing them on the table. "Is there anything else I can get for you ladies?"

"No, everything is fine. Thank you," Maya hurried.

"It sure is," said Elyse, as she pretended to accidentally touch his hand.

"Is there something I can help you with?" he asked patiently, as he quickly moved his hand.

"There is one thing. But it's not for me. It's more for you," she smiled innocently.

"How is that?" he reluctantly asked.

"Do you attend church anywhere around here?"

"No, actually I'm new to the area."

"Well, there's a really good church that you can attend. It's right around the corner. We all go there. It's called Liberty Church. Sunday service starts at 11:00 a.m."

"Okay, I'll keep that in mind," he said, while looking at me. "I haven't seen you here before. Are you new to the area, too?"

"Yes, I am," I said quietly.

"That's good. Then I'm not the only newbie in town."

"Guess not," said Elyse, obviously annoyed that he had switched his attention to someone else. He smiled at me and went to the next table and started taking their order. We finished eating and got up to leave. As we walked out the door, Jeffrey caught my eye.

"Are you going to church on Sunday, Carmen?"

"Yes, I'll be there," I nodded.

"Then I might just show up, too," he grinned.

Elyse overheard and couldn't hide her excitement. "Cool, I'll save a seat for you," she said excitedly, still obviously flirting.

"Make sure it's in the back," he called, then turned to head back to work.

That night when I put Marilyn to bed, I prayed over her like I normally did until she fell asleep. I tried to go to sleep in her room, but for some reason I was restless. I walked toward my bedroom door, but I couldn't bring myself to open the door. I turned around and went into the living room to watch TV and lay on the couch. I finally fell asleep around midnight, but I tossed and turned until I was awakened by voices in my head. *"You like it don't you? Keep liking it! Ain't that right, Carmen? 'Cause you know your uncle loves you. No other special niece is as special to me. Happy you'll be. You gone be so happy. Stop whining like a little girl. Be quiet! Don't tell anyone. You like it, don't you? Give me your hand!"*

I woke in a cold sweat, only to see a man standing right in front of me....

CONTROL

Elyse had an issue with controlling other people. She did not trust God to bless her with what she desired, so she took matters into her own hands. The result was years of emptiness and bitterness. Because Elyse did not have a genuine relationship with the Lord, she did not put her needs and desires in His hands for Him to supply them. Instead, she was too busy trying to control every situation herself. She lacked the faith to believe that whatever she asked for in Jesus' name would be given to her. Elyse was not following God's messages that were continually being delivered to her heart and mind. She was full of fear and didn't believe in God's words to her. She didn't believe that God could and would help her. Elyse's loudness was a facade that replaced her insecurity because of her lack of trust in God to meet her every need.

Any form of control or manipulation is witchcraft. Never allow fear, insecurity, or impatience to take you to the wrong side to seek answers. *God* is a rewarder to those who diligently seek *Him.* His best for you will come in His timing, not yours. Sometimes we are not ready for what we are asking Him for. It is not that God is saying 'no'. Often, He is saying, "Wait. Let me prepare your heart, mind, and spirit for what you are asking for." Ask God to help you discern, learn, and understand His processes and timing.

Delight yourself also in the Lord, and He will give you the desires and secret petitions of your heart. Psalms 37:4 - (AMP)

Chapter Fifteen

I'LL REPENT TOMORROW

"Carmen, it's morning. Time to get up, Sweets," Langston said as he stroked my forehead softly.

"Langston, it's been so long since you've been home. So much has happened."

"I know, but you're still the only woman that I love, and that's all that matters."

I didn't exactly know what he meant by that. I had mixed emotions. On one hand I was relieved he was home. On the other hand, I had no idea what happened when he was away. One thing I did know for sure, I didn't want him touching me!

"So Carmen, what have you been up to since I've been gone?" he asked, snuggling up to me on the couch.

"I joined Liberty Church. It's a small church down the way, just a few blocks from the house."

"You joined a church?"

"Yes, and I'm sure you will love it."

"What kind of church is it?"

"It's a really good church."

"I mean is it a Methodist church or a Baptist church?"

"No, it's neither."

"Don't tell me it's one of those churches where people get really loud and start shouting, speaking in tongues and carrying on."

"Langston!"

"Well, what do you expect? I wasn't raised like that, with women always running through the pews and sweatin' like men. It's just not natural."

"That's because God is moving on them."

"Moving on them? It looks like they've lost their minds, especially right after they open their eyes and look right at you. Talk about scary," he grumbled and faked a shiver.

"I thought you weren't afraid of anything?"

"Who said I was afraid?"

"It's really not that bad."

"Really? Then if God is moving on them as you say, why can't He also move their hair?"

"What are you talking about?"

"I'm just saying, a woman's hair is her glory. But after all that sweating and shouting — well, no wonder there's so many single women in the church."

"That's not very nice, Langston."

"Baby, that's how men think. It has nothing to do with being nice. It's just the way we think is all."

"The church is Pentecostal."

"Penta what?" his confusion clearly showed on his forehead as he looked at me.

"Pentecostal. You'll see what I'm talking about once we go to service tonight."

"Carmen, I just got home. I'm not up to going to no church tonight."

"Please, Langston? I told the Pastor and the Pillars of Praise all about you."

"Who and what are the Pillars of Praise? This church of yours sure has some strange names."

"They're the praise and worship leaders at the church."

"Is the Pastor going to make me stand up to have a few words? I'm not into all that."

"I'm not sure, but he's been praying for our family ever since I joined the church."

"That's good of him. I'm glad they have been taking care of you in my absence. I guess I should go at least once, to see where you've been spending all your time."

"Okay."

I was so happy Langston agreed to go to the service. I knew that once he visited Liberty Church he would love it just as much as I did. I couldn't wait for the Holy Spirit to move on him so he could feel the touch of God like I had. Once we arrived at church, all eyes were on Langston. I felt a little uneasy. Elyse walked up to us before service started and began talking to him.

"Hey there handsome. You must be Carmen's beef on a stick."

"Pardon me?" Langston asked, taken aback by her shameless comment.

"Don't you see my wife and daughter standing right here?"

"I mean, you must be Carmen's husband, right?" Elyse cooed.

"Yes, I am her husband," Langston replied defensively.

"Okay, okay. Don't be so testy. Just making conversation before the service starts. Carmen, why didn't you tell a sister your husband was so good looking? You got a brother, Langston?"

Afraid of what she might do next, I told Marilyn to go sit on the third row pew, our normal seat. The pastor walked toward us. I thanked God that he did.

"Praise the Lord, Sister Carmen. Is this your husband?"

"Yes Pastor, this is my husband, Langston."

All the while, Elyse was staring at Langston like he was a T-bone steak, licking her lips, and shaking her right leg.

"Well, praise God. It's a pleasure to finally meet you. We've been praying for your safe return. Welcome home, son. Welcome home. Enjoy the service, and if there's anything you and your family need, just let the ministry know."

"Thank you, Pastor. I appreciate the hospitality."

"No problem, son. That's what we're here for."

Elyse walked in between Langston and I, then joyously said, "Remember what the Pastor said. Just let me know if there's anything that you need or want and it's yours."

Langston stepped away from her and took my hand, and we went to sit down. The choir began to sing. I could tell Langston was enjoying himself because he was tapping his right leg to the music, and he clapped occasionally, too. Marilyn was so happy that he was there that she was beaming with excitement. It was such a joy for us to be in church as a family. I stroked his hand and thanked God for bringing my husband home to us.

"Praise the Lord, brothers and sisters," said the pastor, speaking to the congregation.

"Praise the Lord, Pastor."

"It is indeed a blessing to be in the presence of the saints."

"Amen. Hallelujah! Absolutely!"

"God has smiled on us once again by bringing home the beloved husband of our dear sister, Carmen."

"Thank you, Jesus," Elyse shouted out loudly. The whole congregation practically turned around to look at her. Maya whispered from across the room for her to be quiet.

"Sister Carmen, would you and your husband like to share a few words?"

I started to rise from my seat, but Langston tugged me back into place, urging me not to.

"No thank you, Pastor," Langston said.

"Well son, I just want to take this time to say thank you for visiting our church. Remember, you and your lovely family will continually remain in our prayers, and if there's anything you need, just ask."

"Thank you, Pastor. We appreciate that."

"That's what we're here for, son. We're here to pray for the families God has so graciously put together. For whosoever God hath joined together, let no man put asunder."

Langston nudged me again and whispered in my ear, "How long does church last?"

"About two hours."

"I can't wait that long!"

"You can't wait that long for what?"

"Carmen, I've been gone six months," Langston whispered almost urgently. Then he softly kissed my ear, but I pulled away stunned and annoyed.

"Langston, we're in church." I couldn't believe him. What was he thinking? But then again, I knew what he was thinking. I became so irritated that I know it showed on my face throughout the service. I knew all he was thinking about was sex!

How could he think about sex while the pastor was preaching?

"I said, what God hath joined together, let no man put asunder."

"See Carmen, even the pastor knows what we should be doing right now--flesh to flesh and bone to bone."

"You are quoting the Scriptures incorrectly, and you are distracting me from hearing the Word," I said, irritated at his fleshly mindset.

"But if you're single, you've got to wait. Wait on Him," the pastor continued.

"Why should I have to wait anymore, Carmen? The wait is over, Sweets! It's time to knock some boots."

"Wait on the Lord to bless you with a mate," the pastor said.

I turned to Langston, "Just wait. It won't be too much longer."

The pastor continued, "Wait on the Lord to honor your faithfulness."

"Yes, sir. Preach it preacher!" the congregation chimed.

"Can I get an amen?"

"Amen!"

"Can I get a wait?"

"Wait!"

"Can I get a wait on Him?"

"Wait on Him."

"And when God gives you a husbandman...."

"Mmm hmmm."

"I said when God gives you a husband, that husband will take care of you for the rest of your life."

"Preach on, preacher!"

"He'll work for you!"

"Yessss!"

"He'll provide for you."

"Mmm hmmm."

"When God gives you a husband, He knows what you need, when you need it."

"Amen, Pastor," Langston agreed.

"Glory, hallelujah," said Elyse as she fanned herself like she was about to pass out from the excitement of the sermon--or maybe it was from the heat. It was hard to tell.

"And that's why you've got to wait. Wait, I say. Wait on the Lord and He will…. Can you say, "He will?"

"He will. He will. He will. Glory to God! He will!"

"He will strengthen your heart. Oh yes, He will."

While the pastor was preaching, a woman in the first pew suddenly started screaming and jumping up and down like the Holy Spirit had moved her in a mighty way. Marilyn giggled, but Langston became uncomfortable and was immediately ready to leave.

"It's time to go," he insisted.

"Okay," I surrendered.

As we got up to leave, Elyse and Bridget waved good night to us, but then Elyse followed us outside into the humid night air. I immediately put Marilyn in the car.

"Leaving so soon, Carmen?"

I was irritated that she came out after us.

"Yes, Langston just got home."

"Oh, I understand. After being gone for such a long time, I'm sure Langston has more on his mind than church," she snickered.

Langston laughed a bit under his breath, too.

"Sure is hot out here, ain't it Langston?" Elyse said.

"Yes, it is a bit warm," he replied.

"Warm, hot, and sweaty. Makes for good...."

Not giving her a chance to say anything else, Langston interrupted. "Excuse us. Sweets, let's go."

"Sweets? He calls you sweets?"

"Yes, that's my nickname for her," he smiled.

"That sure is cute. But I can be just as sweet."

I was thrown completely off by her. This time she had gone too far. I couldn't believe those words came from her lips, even with as much as I'd gotten to know her. She was actually coming onto Langston, with me standing right there. I just looked at her with fury in my eyes.

"Goodbye, Elyse," I scoffed.

"See you later. Remember, you can always stop by. You know the address---555 Blake Street. Hope to see you soon, now. Bye!" she turned and walked back into the church. We walked to the car.

"You didn't tell me about Elyse," Langston commented.

"What about Elyse?"

He shrugged his shoulders. "It's nothing," he said quickly. "How many other friends do you have at that church?"

"About three more--Bridget, Maya, and Keith."
"Who's Keith?"

"He's the minister of music. He was the one playing the piano tonight."

"So, were they...what did you call them?"

"The Pillars of Praise," I reminded him.

"Even Elyse?"

"Yes, even Elyse."

It was obvious that Elyse had gotten his attention. But then again, she always had a habit of catching people off guard, so I didn't think anything of it. Langston drove home, and I laid my head back on the seat and closed my eyes. By the time we got home I was really tired. I quickly jumped into the shower so I could wind all the way down. A hot shower was exactly what I needed, but then I heard the bathroom door open. The next thing I knew, Langston was in the shower with me.

"What are you doing?" I screeched.

"Can't a man take a shower with his wife?" he smiled with his pearly whites.

I immediately thought about the shower I took right after he left.

"Langston, I'm tired. I just want to take a shower and go to bed."

"That's exactly what I want to do. Finally, we're on the same page." He proceeded to pull me toward him and kissed me on my neck.

"I mean, I need to go to sleep," I sharply said.

"Go to sleep? Carmen, it's been six long months. You look so beautiful. I just want to be with you tonight like it's our first time."

"Langston, I'm really tired, and I don't have three bars of soap."

He looked at me with a puzzled gaze, and I couldn't believe I'd said that out loud. What would he think? How could I possibly explain? I thought to myself.

"Three bars of soap? What are you talking about?"

"It's just...I'm so tired, and I need to get some sleep."

He blew out his breath and stepped out of the shower. He took his towel, wrapped it around himself, and left the bathroom, dripping wet. I could hear him mumbling to himself. "I can't believe my own wife keeps rejecting me. You would think that after six months, she'd show a brother some love."

Even though I heard him, I didn't respond to what he was saying. How could I? I stayed in the bathroom for a little while longer, until I thought he had fallen asleep. I got into the bed softly, and quietly said, "Good night." I assumed he was asleep because he didn't say anything. I quickly dozed off.

****

Knock, knock, knock.

"Who is it?" Elyse asked.

"It's Langston."

"Langston? Carmen's Langston?"

"Yes, it's me."

"What are you doing here?"

"I was thinking about what you said."

"What exactly was that?"

"I was contemplating sleeping with you, but you flirted with me right in front of my wife, which is downright disrespectful."

"Well, sleeping with me is the best thing that will ever happen to you!"

"I came over to tell you never to do that again. I was tempted by your advances, but I love my wife too much to be enticed by you."

"Then why show up in the first place, sending me mixed signals and smelling all good?"

"Like I said, I will not be drawn into your web of lust!"

"Once you touch me, you'll be addicted."

"Addicted to what?"

"Me of course!"

"Well, that's not gonna happen."

"What makes you so sure about that?"

"I would never choose you over my wife. You got that?!"

"Yeah, yeah," she said, shaking her head and rolling her eyes.

"No, you really don't."

Langston's love for me overshadowed his temporary attraction to Elyse as he realized there must be something going on with me that I had not shared with him.

"What do you mean?" Elyse persisted.

"I'm making it clear to you that I love my wife. Goodnight." Langston returned home to find me still sleeping. He moved closer to me. Suddenly I awoke to find him sitting on the bed. He looked into my eyes.

"What's wrong Langston?"

"Carmen, I love you so much. I need to tell you something."

I took a deep breath and sat up to listen to what he had to say.

"I went to see Elyse at her house. Honestly, I was tempted by her flirting with me; but I overcame the temptation because I love you and realized that there must be a reason why being with me is difficult for you."

For the first time, I felt my husband's pain, and tears welled up in my eyes. I started to cry.

"Langston, I know that I have not been fair to you. I must tell you something. Please forgive me for not telling you before we got married. I was molested by my uncle at the age of seven and raped by a boy when I was a teenager. That's when I got pregnant. I never told anyone who the father was. You deserve someone who can truly be a wife to you. I love you but, I am unable to express it physically."

"Carmen, it's not your fault. I would never..."

"No, let me finish. It's wrong for you to have to beg me to make love to you. I was reading a book about what happens to a person when they are violated. They either become frigid and totally shut down, or they become addicted to sex. I think God has given me the best husband, and I am just messed up. I want to be your wife in every sense of the word. I do not want to lose you. I just need....Will you help me? I believe we will be okay. I just hope it's not too late."

Langston rose from the bed with tears in his eyes. He began to pace back and forth from one side of the room to the other. He paused and looked at me as I threw the covers back to reveal a sexy gown I had been saving for him.

"Carmen!" Amazed by my sudden surprise, he slowly approached the bed and whispered in my ear. "I wish you had told me."

Looking deeply into his eyes, I reached out to him and we embraced.

"Carmen darling, you are so beautiful!"

"Langston, I think I'm ready now...for real this time.

CHOICE

Early in our marriage, Langston's conscience convicted him, but he acted contrary to what he knew was right, only to wake up the next morning feeling terrible about what he had done to himself and his wife. Despite the fact that he knew the Word of God, he ended up right where he knew he shouldn't be. Langston chose to act on the desires he had for sex outside of his covenant love relationship with Carmen. The weakness of Langston's sexual nature drove him into the arms of other women who enticed him and captivated his attention; but he learned from his mistakes and truly repented.

Do not allow unholy desires to dictate your future. Put your flesh under submission to God and do what you know is right. If you're having trouble in a particular area, contact your pastor or mentor and let him or her know what you are struggling with before you make the mistake. Instant gratification can lead to self-destruction and broken relationships. Making the right choices in life is not always easy; but making poor choices with intentions of repenting later is not a godly way of managing your life. Tomorrow is not guaranteed to anyone. Every one of us should have a pastor or godly mentor to guide us through the overwhelming times in our lives that are inevitable regardless of how carefully we plan our course.

For the wages which sin pays is death, but the [bountiful] free gift of God is eternal life through (in union with) Jesus Christ our Lord. Romans 6:23 - (AMP)

Chapter Sixteen

IF GOD GAVE ME A HUSBAND

Seven years had gone by and Elyse was still flirting with Langston at church. She continued to insult me right in front of him. One afternoon at church, she started her put-downs.

"When are you going to drop that 'potato'? You sure are big. If I got pregnant and looked like you, I would just die! Matter of fact, why don't you just keel over so I can get mine? I'm just saying. I deserve him, not you!"

I was fuming inside. I was so upset. I could feel my temperature rising and steam building up from my frontal lobe. How could she?! One of these days I was going to tell her a thing or two. She was making me so mad, but she just kept on.

"What does it feel like to be ready to pop, or should I say *explode* and then sag? You've had so many already I've lost count. You must feel like you're carrying the mother lode." She was laughing in a lame attempt to be funny and insulting me at the same time.

"Wow! Pretty soon you're gonna have your own little choir--Generation X Pillars of Praise Incorporated. Hey! Can I get a witness?" she jeered while jumping, shaking, and bobbing her head like she was dancing in the spirit.

"Whatever God has planned for my children is alright with me," I said.

"My man doesn't go for nothing like that," Elyse said, twisting her hands about and moving her neck from side to side. "I have to make sure I stay on top of my game."

"What game?" I asked her innocently.

"The game of woman verses woman," she triumphantly pronounced. "If you don't look good for your man, some other woman will."

"That's your opinion! The last time I checked, you were single and had to use tricks just to get a man. I never have to worry about that. Langston adores me and the way I look." I was sick and tired of her rude remarks, and I lashed out at her. I knew better, but there were times when I just couldn't help myself.

"Well, a woman has to do what a woman has to do. I have needs. If a man is not getting what he needs at home, it's not my fault when he comes to me. I remember when a man I know told me that a woman should always look her best--from the crown of her head to the soles of her feet. His pet peeve was a woman's unkempt hair. One time he said that a woman shouted so hard she sweated her weave right off her head. He wondered what god she was serving, because his God was a God of order, and there was nothing orderly about that. He said her hair was standing up all over her head."

"Elyse, don't even try to insinuate that Langston told you that. He tells me constantly that I'm beautiful."

"Well, that's never been a problem with me. I don't need anyone to tell me that as you can see. I already know."

I had a hard time keeping a pleasant disposition as she continued to run her mouth about how much weight I had gained.

"You look like you weigh 200 pounds."

"Well, I am pregnant."

"What does that have to do with anything? Carmen, you've got a fine husband, and I do mean *fine*! But you sure don't know what to do with him. If God gave me a husband like that, he would never leave the house."

"Elyse, what are you talking about?"

"You see, there are two ways to get a man to stay home. One—cooking, and two—cooking. I know how to put the motion in the waves to make a man think he's at sea, when all the time he's just with me. That, my dear Carmen, will make a man stay home."

"Elyse, you don't even have a man."

"How do you know what I have? You're not in my bed! I give my man what he needs, and he gives me what I love. When was the last time Langston stayed home?"

"What do you mean? He's at home every night."

"Are you sure about that?"

"Yes, of course I am." I ignored her obvious attempt to bring me down to her level, but the whole time I was fuming on the inside and just wished she would shut up.

Suddenly, the church door swung open and in walked Jeffrey, the waiter from the restaurant. We hadn't seen him in years because he no longer worked at the restaurant. He also had not been at church.

"Hello Jeffrey. You're a fabulous sight to see," Elyse flirted.

"Hi Elyse. How are you? It's been a long time."

"I'm just fine. It's good to see you again. The last time we saw you was at the restaurant seven years ago. What happened to you?"

"Life happened."

"Life happens to everybody, but you disappeared from the planet all together," she smirked.

"I've been here. You just haven't seen me."

"What are you talking about? I've got twenty-twenty vision. If you were here, I would have definitely seen you."

"Not necessarily. You're a talker, not an observer. Besides, I came to see the pastor. I have something I need to talk to him about. I didn't come to see you."

I felt so relieved he had come in. He had a way of silencing her.

"Well, as the pastor's secretary, I should tell you that his schedule is full today. You'll have to call and make an appointment. I have work to do. Excuse me," Elyse said abruptly. She went back into her office, turned the music on, and closed the door behind her. We could see her dancing provocatively through the window.

"Carmen, it's nice to see you again," he said with a smile.

"Thank you, Jeffrey. It's nice to see you also."

"When is your baby due?"

"She's due any day now."

"So you know it's a girl?"

"I have a pretty good feeling," I said, smiling warmly as I softly hugged my big round stomach.

"Oh, okay, woman's intuition. Have you decided on a name for your baby girl yet?"

"We're praying about naming her Courtney."

"That's a lovely name."

"We think so."

"If you ever need any help getting around, just let me know. I'll be happy to come and pick you up. It's not safe for you to drive this close to your due date."

"I'm not driving. My husband will be here soon to pick me up."

"What time will he be here?"

"Around 3 o'clock."

"It's 3:15 right now."

"He's a little late, but I'm sure he'll be here soon."

"I don't understand why he wouldn't be here early to pick you up."

"I'm sure there is a perfect explanation why he isn't here yet. He's always on time."

Langston finally arrived.

"Sweets, it's time to go." He didn't even speak to Elyse or Jeffrey, which I thought was odd. He was usually very polite.

"Okay," I nodded. "We'll see you later, Jeffrey. Make sure you come to service on Sunday. The pastor would love to see you," I said.

Langston and I were walking toward the car when he asked, "When did you meet Jeffrey?"

I wondered why he asked this, but I replied, "At the restaurant with Bridget, Maya, and Elyse. Elyse invited him to church. He told us he'd be coming to service. We just didn't know when. That was years ago."

"Anytime you see him coming, I want you to go in the opposite direction."

"What?" I looked at Langston strangely, surprised by his jealousy.

"I don't want you to see or talk to him again."

"I don't understand. Why not?"

"Trust me. I know his kind."

"You just saw him for the first time."

"I know men. Get in the car. I'll be right back."

He turned back to say something to Jeffrey, then abruptly walked back to the car.

"Okay, Sweets. Let's go," he said, clearing his throat.

CONTENTMENT

Elyse was a lonely soul who needed someone to control. She couldn't be happy with herself because she didn't love herself. She didn't know what it was like to have a man who really loved her, nor did she allow God to show her His love. She had her own personal agenda all worked out. She didn't realize it would soon backfire on her. If she would have just waited on the Lord, she would have been blessed. Instead, she got impatient and missed out on God's plan for her life.

God lets us know in his Word that He has plans for us, and those plans are to bless and protect us. We can have hope. Even when things don't seem to be working out the way we plan, God is in control, and He knows our future. Often, we see people with similar behaviors as Elyse's and wonder what has occurred in their lives to cause them to behave as they do. Elyse felt unloved by those around her. Therefore, she needed to control them. God had given her a powerful ability to get others to follow her. It was a God-given gift. She was a born leader. However, she was not using her gift for the One who gave it to her. If she had just sought relationship with the Lover of her soul, she would have known she was loved and would have received her heart's desires.

But seek (aim at and strive after) first His kingdom and His righteousness (His way of doing and being right), and then all these things taken together will be given you besides. Matthew 6:33 - (AMP)

Chapter Seventeen

LET ME INTRODUCE YOU

Ten years later I received a phone call from a woman I knew nothing about, except her name. Her voice on the phone was kind, but what she revealed was shocking.

"Elyse is going around telling people that she is in a relationship with Langston. You seem like a nice lady, and I am telling you this because she did the same thing to me. She carries the cloak of deception and cannot be trusted."

"I don't want to hear anymore. My nerves cannot stand this." I immediately hung up the phone. My knees buckled, and I hit the floor. My heart started racing. I lost all control of my mind, wondering if what the woman said was true! I literally flipped out and decided to do something about what I pondered in my mind. I began to plot how I would take my own life. I pulled out a piece of paper and started to write. I wrote down exactly when and where I would do it. I wrote down the time of day and the place. It was as if I couldn't stop writing, planning, and looking forward to ending my life. I wrote continuously until my hand was exhausted. I was possessed to my own ruin. Three hours later I was still writing. Thank God my kids were at my mother's house. I had finally snapped to a point that when I looked at myself in the mirror, my reflection was a face I had never seen before. I was in a terrible state of mind. Just then I heard the front door open.

"Hey Sweets. How you doing?"

"How do you think I'm doing? I just got off the phone with Misty."

"Who is Misty?" He denied knowing her.

"You know exactly who she is! Don't pretend that you don't. She's another one of your women," I ranted.

"You're my only woman, Sweets."

"Sweets! Don't even go there. I can't take it any longer. You are not the man I thought you were."

"Carmen, you need to calm down."

"Calm down? Calm down? I will not calm down! You are playing around!"

"Now you're talking crazy."

"Crazy? I'll show you crazy!"

I ran toward the kitchen and opened the kitchen drawer with all the knives. I pulled out the biggest knife I could get my hands on and ran back into the living room. My handwritten plans changed in that moment from taking my life to taking his.

"You see this knife, Langston?" I screamed. "It's got your name on it! I'm goanna finally give you what you deserve."

Langston stepped backward and started toward the door. I could see the fear in his eyes.

"You look scared, Langston. Where are you going? I got something for you. Come here and let me wipe that *'you're the only woman I'll ever love'* look off your face."

"I thought you were a Christian."

"Oh, so that makes you think you can run over me and do what you want when you want? I beg to differ, Langston. It's time for you to meet your Maker. Let me introduce you! Jesus, Langston

Alexander is headed toward the pearly gates, or should I say the gates of hell! The blood of Jesus is against you brotha! Here comes a special delivery long overdue," I yelled, lunging towards him.

Langston bolted out the front door, and I ran after him. I slipped and fell because I was in heels, and it was raining outside. I quickly got up with the knife still in my hand. I was bleeding from somewhere, but I did not care.

I went back into the house and grabbed my keys. I didn't think I would ever see Langston again. I'd lost all hope for us. I was at my wits end. I ran to my car and drove off quickly. I drove for what seemed like hours. As it began to rain even harder, I could barely see the road. I kept driving with no destination in mind. While I drove, what little mind I had left wanted to die. Suddenly, I heard a familiar voice. It was the same voice I heard on that beautiful sunny day when my uncle called me into the house and my body was violated as a child. I could no longer be rational. I was being controlled by the devil's plan to take my own life. The devil said for me to press on the accelerator until it hit the floor and then let go of the steering wheel. I closed my eyes and imagined I was dead. My last thought was that everyone who had ever hurt me would be sorry. Something evil had grown in my heart, and it made me want to get even.

Vindictive and absorbed by bitterness, taking my own life appeared to be an easy way out. With my spirit deeply laced in spite and hatred, getting even at any cost had become my obsession. I had become selfish and didn't consider how killing

myself would affect those who loved me--
especially my children. My heart was callous
because of the pain I had suppressed for years. I
wanted others to feel that same pain. Suddenly, I
heard tires squealing and the commotion of heavy
freeway traffic.

Miraculously I sustained no harm as I realized
I had come to a complete stop right on the freeway
exit. It could have only been an angel of the Lord
who lifted my car across four lanes of traffic on
the I-80 freeway and placed me softly on the
freeway shoulder. I knew an angel had carried me
through my deepest and darkest hour and had
saved my life. Then, I heard the voice of
deliverance call my name.

"Carmen."

"Yes, Lord."

His voice was soft yet powerful.

"Carmen, if you do not want to live any longer,
then live for Me. Give your testimony to other
women to let them know that when nobody else
cares, I do. I want you to trust Me. I will take care
of you, but you must trust Me. The first thing you
need to do is forgive."

When the Lord spoke those words to me, I
couldn't believe what I was hearing.

"Who me? Forgive what, Lord?"

"That which has caused you to become bitter."

"How can I?" I questioned.

"I will teach you how."

I had a burst on the inside of me that made me
feel like living again. I began to cry with tears of
deliverance because I knew then that even though
I felt horribly disappointed, my life now had a
purpose to help other women who were also going

through the same or similar things. I wiped away the tears from my eyes, caught my breath, and drove back to the house to wait for Langston to come home. I waited well into the night, but he didn't return until after I had gotten into bed. When he came home, he made an extra effort to ensure he didn't disturb me by softly lying beside me. I had made up in my mind to forgive him, knowing how I had held myself from being a wife to him for so long. Also, what if he did have an affair because I secretly wished he had someone else for that part?

The break in my heart would be a test of my faith and my trust in God. Even though I did not feel forgiveness in my heart, the Lord told me to just forgive him. I came to realize that forgiveness is an act of faith. It is not based on feelings. I was determined to follow God's will, so I began learning how to forgive. The next morning we didn't say much to each other. I made breakfast for him like I normally did, and he sat down to eat. He would always say that he enjoyed the meal, and that morning was no exception.

"I see you've cooled down," he said afterward.

I thought I would be able to face him, but I couldn't. I just turned from him and went upstairs to our room. Suddenly, the phone rang and Langston answered it from downstairs. I couldn't resist picking up the other extension to listen in. What I heard made me very ill. I began vomiting loudly and uncontrollably. Langston ran upstairs.

"What's wrong with you?"

"I heard you on the phone saying you think I need to talk to my pastor. You don't know what to do because I am saying things that aren't true. All this is too much! I'm sick to my stomach and feel dizzy. I need to go to the doctor."

He tried to lift me up, but I was too upset and rejected his help.

"You don't have to take me," I said. "I'll drive myself." I pulled myself together, got into the car, and left the house. When I arrived at the doctor's office a man in a white coat walked into the room. It was as if he knew exactly what was going on in my life by the words he spoke to me.

"Carmen, you are a beautiful and intelligent woman, but you have allowed someone to cause you to be insecure. I never want to see you here again because of this. Don't allow anyone to bring you to this point. You need to rise and know who you are. Release what has you in bondage so you can really live. You have so much to offer, but you have so much fear." This was yet another divine visitation. I knew this man was another angel of God. Something was ignited inside of me, and I began to feel like there was hope for me after all.

I realized then that the perception I had of myself had been based on so many lies because of the twisted needs of others to control me. However, as the years went by, I still believed I was blessed just to have a husband, especially a good man like Langston. I felt unattractive and homely and was afraid to say anything to him about my insecurity. Because I was being controlled by a spirit of fear, things only got worse after I shared my past experiences with my husband. It caused a blanket of shame to hover over me. But being the good man that he was, Langston never brought up my deepest secrets that caused me to be insecure. There was no reason for me to be suspicious.

Although we had marital problems, we both loved our children and strove to protect them. Langston was a model father and a good provider for the family. My lack of communication with him and my inability to perform as often as he desired, is what caused friction in our marriage. It seemed like every time we were intimate, I got pregnant. I barely had time to process one emotion before I was hit with the next! I had three nervous breakdowns because I was holding on to the pain and the trauma of my youth. Langston asked me to talk to a doctor, but I was too ashamed. The cultural stigma of therapy was a voice that would not allow me to seek counsel. It put me in a viscous cycle of endless entrapment. Each time I would pray and ask God to help me, I just couldn't give myself over to my husband. The one thing I did know, however, is that for me to move forward, I had to learn how to forgive Langston from my heart. Even though I no longer trusted him, I fully learned the value of forgiveness as we continued to live together and truly love one another.

Once I was truly able to forgive, we became the best of friends. We had a date every Friday night. Langston made special arrangements to get off early from work on Fridays so we could spend quality time together. We went to many different restaurants for dinner and enjoyed each other's company. Langston also strove to make our family stronger by planning annual vacations for us and making sure we maintained strong relationship ties at church. One thing Langston really loved to do was sing, and I encouraged him to produce a CD. His daughters also believed in his golden voice and paid to have his CD produced, entitled *"This is It!"*.

Even though we were making progress in our marriage, I still had a fear of getting hurt. Honestly, I didn't trust anyone with my heart. I just couldn't bring myself to that point, no matter how hard I tried. My husband and I came to live a peaceful life and had lots of fun together because we both liked to travel and experience new things. He tried very hard to make things better, but it seemed there was nothing he could do to get me to truly trust him with my whole heart. Langston believed that God joined us together. He believed there was nothing that could separate us.

Today, I also believe that whatsoever God joins together in holy matrimony, no man can separate. The one thing I discovered throughout the difficulties we experienced in our marriage was the strength of our friendship. The catalyst of our friendship was at the root of us staying together.

One day Langston and I were talking, and he revealed to me that his mother had left him when he was only two years old.

"To this day, I yearn for the affection of my mother and continually grieve for the love relationship we never had. There is a missing piece within me that needs to be healed," he confided one day.

After he shared this with me, I felt totally unworthy of his love because of how I had treated him. The rejection he experienced at such a tender age from the person who was supposed to love and protect him the most was unfortunately repeated when I also rejected him as his wife. Langston needed time and attention filled with patience and genuine love for him. It was then that I stepped out of my comfort zone and did the unthinkable.

"Langston..." I hesitated.

"Yes." I was at a loss for words, but my actions were worth more than a thousand. I willingly embraced him with tears in my eyes and held onto him for dear life!

"That was real," he said with a joyous shout! Little did we know that our season of freedom and forgiveness would soon fade into a time of uncertainty.

SELF CONTROL

Carmen did not have control of her emotions and it was an open door for a big attack from the enemy. Satan used Carmen's emotional turmoil as a weapon against her. Long before she came into the realization and understanding of her God-ordained purpose, she was already a threat to the kingdom of darkness, so Satan wanted to take her life!

Self-control is a fruit of the Holy Spirit. Sometimes life becomes so overwhelming that in impatience we take matters into our own hands and try to solve problems the wrong way. This will always make the situation worse. We must be careful not to be carried away in a moment by our own emotions, even when someone deliberately does or says something to make us upset. We must realize that we are not fighting flesh and blood, but principalities, powers, and rulers in high places (Ephesians 6:12). We are in a *spiritual* battle. Therefore, take it to God and refuse to fight it in the flesh. God expects us to solve conflicts in a peaceful manner, being full of the fruits of the Spirit (Galatians 5:22-23). God will help us through conflict if we listen to His voice and follow His plan.

The Lord will fight for you, and you shall hold your peace and remain at rest. Exodus 14:14 - (AMP)

Renewing of our vows on our 38th anniversary

Chapter Eighteen

THE HELP-MEET

Years passed and God was faithful to bring increasing love and understanding into our marriage and home. We renewed our wedding vows and committed ourselves to being a model couple for other marriages that were struggling as we once had. Then suddenly, it was as if a bomb hit our home. Langston came home from the doctor with news that he was terminally ill.

The season of my husband's sickness would soon consume me with caring for him as well as our family. I had to maintain the lifestyle we had become accustomed to, or at least, I did not want my husband to have to worry about money anymore. God had blessed us with a very attractive and comfortable home. I began to work endless hours at the church God gave us. I also started travelling extensively and found myself speaking and encouraging others at various churches. God, our Provider made sure the bills were always paid on time. No one knew how much of a struggle it was, but God saw us through. I increasingly tried to reassure Langston of my love through my actions. I was so sorry that the abuse of my childhood had kept me from being the woman and wife he needed me to be for so long. Still, he loved me unconditionally with his forgiving spirit.

One evening while he was resting, he took my hand.

"I am sorry, Carmen."

"Why are you apologizing?" I asked. "You can't help that you're sick. Stop talking like that. You're going to be alright," I insisted, not wanting to face the truth. He broke down and cried. His repeated words echoed loudly in my head. 'Carmen, always remember that you're the only woman I've ever really loved.'

I was in a daze. We had been together for such a long time and living without him never even entered my mind. After we talked, he went to sleep and I silently cried out to God.

"Lord, I knew the time would come when you would call Langston home, but please God, give us a little more time together. Lord, he's the husband you gave me. He's a good father. He's a good provider. He takes care of us. Lord God, please don't take him now! Don't take him. Don't take him now! Please God, don't take him!"

I felt like my heart had stopped beating. As I prayed, I recalled our first date that seemed so long ago.

"Why are you calling me Sweets?" I asked.

"Because to me there's nothing sweeter than you," he answered.

"How do you know that? You don't even know me that well."

"I know that you are one of the sweetest girls around," he said to me with a warm smile and such kindness in his eyes.

I heard myself laughing in response.

"How many girls do you know?"

"Enough to know that you're not like any of them, and I can't wait until we're married."

The sound of my children's voices pulled me back into the present. When I came to myself, the girls were also by his side, along with our grandchildren. The time had come for the Lord to take Langston home.

I was comforted by the words of a song God gave us to sing to Langston before he was called home. However, it didn't change the fact that I was now alone for the first time in my life. Langston was gone forever. I would no longer see his face or hear his laugh. I would no longer smell the cologne on his skin or touch his brow. I would no longer feel his arms wrapped around me, willing to protect me. My husband was gone, and I was alone. I could not help but weep.

RESPONSIBILITY

The things my husband taught me over the years were priceless because they helped me know how to maintain our household and finances when he became sick. Suddenly, I had to take a solo role. I found myself being forced to do so many things that my husband always took care of. Sometimes we don't appreciate what others around us are doing to make our lives easier until they are no longer there to do it.

One thing I took for granted was that my husband always drove me everywhere. I never had to drive. He would drive me to the mall to shop and was always so patient as I took my time browsing through store after store. Now suddenly, he was sick and I found myself needing to get to a meeting in Sacramento, a three hour drive from my home. I had to drive. My husband gently instructed me to just stay in my lane, no matter what was happening around me. His instructions took me to my meeting and back safely and without incident. He said he was proud of me and that he knew I had it in me. My husband's continual encouragement was the catalyst I needed to push through during his time of illness. He once told my daughter, "I don't know what your mother is doing, but she's doing a really good job."

The biggest encouragement came in the place of ministry. In the early years it was not easy for women, especially women of color to break out into ministry. My husband always told me I was called and that no other person had the right to tell me I shouldn't be a pastor. He explicitly said to me, "You are called to this. If any man tells you that you are not supposed to be doing this, tell him your husband has given you permission to do it. Never stop ministering because God has called you."

The difficult things that come to your life are often God's avenue to get you to a greater place of self-discovery and achievement--*just stay in your lane!* Do not focus on the difficult things or let distractions overtake you. Ask God to show you His purpose in them and allow Him to mold and shape you into a vessel that is increasingly useful in His hands.

"And the Lord God said, 'It is not good that the man should be alone. I will make him a help meet for him.'" Genesis 2:18 –(KJV)

Chapter Nineteen

50 YEARS—TO DEATH DO US PART

When we are at our weakest, God in us is at His strongest. It can sound like a cliché, but when it was time to bury my husband, the Lord showed me how much He truly was my Strength.

I had a prophetic conference that was scheduled to take place a few days after Langston's passing. I was overcome with grief and did not want to do the conference. But suddenly, a divine resolve that could only come from God came over me. As if I were being pushed forward by a divine wind, I finished the conference in the midst of making burial plans for my husband. Then the wind stopped, and all I could think of was how I would be able to stand before our family and friends when my heart was in so much pain. I was devastated by Langston's passing. I was at a loss for words. What would I say? I fell on my knees and cried out to God to help me. Once again, the presence of God came into the room and gave me the strength to speak when I had no strength of my own. I can still remember how God carried me through those difficult days. As I stood in the church and looked out over the pews at all the people who had come to say their goodbyes to Langston, I gained strength from knowing that he was loved by so many people, and that he had made peace with God. Some of the well-wishers I knew and some of them I did not, but it still comforted me to see how many lives he had touched. There was so much warmth and love in the room that my heart was in awe, and I thanked God for the peace He had given me in the presence of so many witnesses.

"I want to thank all of you for coming to express your condolences. It is a blessing to see everyone here today. Your very presence is testimony of the love that you have for Langston and my family. I would like to share a few words in remembrance of my husband."

It was so quiet you could hear a pin drop, even though my voice was as a whisper.

"My husband, Langston, was a good provider. He took care of his family. He was a loving man. He was not perfect, but he tried to be. He was always a blessing to others because he would reach out to those in need. He had such a big heart. Our life together had its ups and downs, but all marriages do. We were blessed to share so many years together with our children. Langston was so involved with our grandchildren that he was cherished and recognized as Grandfather of the Year. Our grandchildren thought he was the best grandfather who ever lived. When you remember this day, please remember Langston as the father that loved his family dearly, and the husband that provided a loving home for us. He took care of our needs and made sure we didn't want for anything. We had a lifetime of memories and so many wonderful times together. My family and I would like to thank all of you for coming."

I quietly took my seat as the program continued and the facilitator read what the family had written to those in attendance.

"Perhaps you prayed a prayer or came to pay a call. Perhaps you sent beautiful flowers. If so, we saw them all. Perhaps you sent or spoke kind words as any friend could say. Perhaps you were not there at all, but just thought of us that day. Perhaps you rendered a service unseen, near at hand or from afar. Whatever you did to console the heart, by word or deed or touch--whatever was the kindly part, we thank you, oh so much!"

After hearing the words that we had penned, there was momentary silence and tears of pain. God sent Langston to me, but then God called him away. The night Langston passed away, I thought I was dreaming. I felt strong arms around me. I began struggling to see who was hugging me, but I could not see the face. It was such a strong embrace that I awoke and started talking to myself. I rocked myself back to sleep. About two hours later I was awakened by my son when I heard him enter my room crying. It was obvious that he was overtaken with emotion as he told me, "I think Dad has passed away." I realized later that Langston had come to comfort me one last time with a loving embrace. Sure, our marriage was not the perfect marriage, and our wedding night was a nightmare to the both of us, but Langston was a very patient man. We were blessed with four beautiful children together because God taught me how to freely submit to my husband and not to be afraid to be intimate with him. Like me, Langston also had a child from a previous relationship--a beautiful baby girl named Pamela. She came to live with us when she was twelve years old and completed our happy family.

Langston had great endurance waiting for me so we could both live a full and enjoyable life. I cannot help but reflect on what a patient husband he was. My mother was truly right about her view on life with a sailor. Throughout the going-home service, there was so much joy in my heart for the love expressed for Langston in so many wonderful words as well as deeds. My heart was full of peace, though my eyes were red with grief. The facilitator read, "*When Tomorrow Starts Without Me*".

"When tomorrow starts without me, and I'm not there to see. If the sun should rise and find your eyes are filled with tears for me; I wish so much you wouldn't cry the way you did today, while thinking of the many things we didn't get to say. I know how much you loved me. I know you'll miss me, too. But when tomorrow starts without me, please try to understand, that an angel came and called my name, and took me by the hand. He said my place was already in heaven far above, and that I'd have to leave behind all those I dearly love. But as I turn to walk away, a tear fell from my eye. For all my life, I'd always thought I didn't want to die. I had so much to live for, so much yet to do. It seemed almost impossible that I was leaving you. I thought of all the love we shared, and all the fun we had. If I could relive yesterday, just even for a while, I'd say good-bye and kiss you and maybe see you smile. But then I fully realized that this could never be, for emptiness and memories would take the place of me. And when I thought of worldly things I might miss come tomorrow, I thought of you, and when I did, my heart filled with sorrow. But when I walked through heaven's gates, I felt so much at home. When God looked down and smiled at me, from his great golden throne. He said, 'This is eternity, and all I've promised you. Today your life on earth is past, but here it starts anew. I promised no tomorrow, but today will always last; and since each day is the same day, there is no longing for the past. But you have been faithful, so trusting and true. Though there were times you did some things, you knew you shouldn't do. But you have been forgiven, and now at last you're free. So won't you take my hand and share eternity with me?' So when tomorrow starts without me, don't think we're far apart. For every time you think of me, I'm right here, in your heart."

I embraced my children with all the strength within me during the remainder of the program. The music started to play as I watched each person say their goodbyes to Langston in their own special way. He had so many friends. I was comforted to know that my husband gave enough of himself to others, that they were willing to give of themselves at his death. However, I wasn't prepared for the song that would be sung, as my daughter danced in his memory, but it was uplifting to me. I kept my composure and remained my husband's wife.

INTEGRITY

Langston and Carmen had been through some very trying times, but Carmen remained faithful to her husband and did not give into the temptations she faced. Nothing could change the integrity she possessed.

What are those special, God-given attributes you possess that no one can change? Maybe you are a giver. Maybe you have a deep capacity to love that no one has been able to diminish. Perhaps you have a 'never quit' spirit that has kept you moving toward and reaching goals when others have quit or failed. Thank God for the desire to keep moving no matter what, because it will drive you into the hands of your destiny that has been designed by God.

God instilled a tenacity in me from birth. It is the part of me that no force of darkness has ever been able to kill. Regardless of the evils done against me, I bounced back and achieved everything I set out to do. Quitting is not in my nature. It is not in my spiritual DNA. It is my heart's desire that you allow the Lord to take your negative emotions and nail them to the cross forever. Release every old and useless mindset, tradition, habit, and unhealthy relationship to God. Begin to receive your validation from Him, your Creator. He does not make mistakes.

To continue the right path toward your destiny, it is imperative that you spend time in the Word of God with expectation and patience that God will gently direct you. It is necessary that you continually ask God to help you make Him an integral part of your daily life. He cares about every detail of your life and will surely lead you to the realization of your dreams and goals; but it is up to *you* to make them a reality.

Let integrity and uprightness preserve me, for I wait for and expect You. Psalms 25:21 - (AMP)

Chapter Twenty

THE SUBSTITUTE

After my husband passed, my world changed completely. I was in deep mourning. Well-meaning people tried to encourage me with the reminder that my husband was with the Lord. Although well intended, their words did little to help me through the grieving process. Therefore, when Jeffrey called me several years later and asked me out for dinner, it was a comforting thing. I was lonely. I was in unfamiliar territory and felt so out of place. The kids were all grown. My self-worth was diminishing, and I felt something was missing. I accepted Jeffrey's invitation.

It was a new beginning for the both of us. The more time I spent with him, the more I became joyful once again. We communicated often on and off the phone. I was treading in dangerous territory and wasn't even aware of it. I started to crave his attention and the sound of his voice. I eventually told him my secret. I shared with him that I had a need for him to be completely honest with me, and we drew even closer. Our friendship began to blossom into something much deeper. One day while I was in my boutique, my body came alive. I felt happy and was excited like a seventeen-year-old girl. As time went on, we spent more and more time with one another. He was wonderful to me. I became possessive of him, and it began to frighten him. Then, over time, I began to see the real man. He wanted to take our relationship to a sexual intimacy, which I rejected. He became angry and said we needed a break from each other or he might suffer a stroke! He tried to end the relationship, but the severance wasn't complete.

Regardless of how I felt about Jeffrey ending our romance, I knew I had not allowed myself to go through the grieving process. I had jumped into a substitute relationship to cover the loss of my husband. I knew I was getting into something that wasn't right. I needed closure from the loss of my husband, but I received rejection instead.

One evening as Jeffrey and I sat and talked, I felt inside that it would be the last time we would speak to each other. However, the feeling of rejection led to additional back-and-forth phone calls. We were not kind to one another, to say the least. In my grief, or should I say in my flesh, I was determined to have the last word. I continued to call Jeffrey. I was not happy until I heard his voice. I had placed an irrational value on our communication. I was also addicted to the sound of his voice. When I was unable to reach him, I would fall apart because it made me crave his attention even more.

Then the Lord spoke to me. He said I had accepted a substitute for Him, and it would always leave me empty. The Lord was showing me that it is possible to get so caught up in something that seems so real, yet it is just a web of deception. I was missing a relationship of closeness. I put all my confidence in being able to replace the emptiness I felt inside with a man when my confidence should have been placed solely in the Lord.

My choice to fill the emptiness with what wasn't real finally led me to have an unquenchable thirst for a deeper relationship with God, and it drove me to seek Him even more. One morning I woke around 6:00 a.m. and called Dr. Intisar Shareef, a dear friend of mine. I shared my dilemma with her. She told me I was going to mess around and end up in a mental institution because I was so consumed with finding a substitute for my husband. She said I was allowing a distraction to replace the relationship I had gained with God over the years with a temporal kiss. Dr. Shareef preached long and hard at me until my mind was released from the false sense of security that I had placed in Jeffrey. I wanted him to be what he could never be. The next morning, I went to church and preached one of the most powerful messages in my life.

HEALING

Come to the quick realization that anything in your life that has enslaved you was never from God. I was living in grief because the enemy sent a substitute to take my mind and heart away from God. I am sharing this with you because I don't want any man or woman to get entrapped in a substitute situation like I did. A substitute situation will always blind you to truth. It will always hinder your completeness in God. It will drive you into the path of regret.

The word "regret" does not have the potential to change anything; but it will put you in a state of stagnancy. Nothing will move in your life until you get rid of regret. A regretful state breeds embarrassment and negative behavior. I realize that I had put myself in a compromising situation, but God was gracious enough to grant me peace amid it all. God provided me with an opportunity to shake off the shame and embarrassment of having allowed a substitute to get to me. I had been hard-headed. I wanted self-gratification during my grief to medicate the emptiness I felt inside.

I know now that the pain I experienced happened for a reason. It brought healing to my spirit when I decided to gradually release my longing for Langston. It was important for me to understand that anything that comes into your life to cover up something else is indeed a substitute. God does not allow flaws in your life just for the sake of having them there. Do not ignore the warning signs God gives you when you are treading in dangerous territory. Do not ignore red flags. Stop making excuses for the inadequacies of a substitute that has taken root in your life as a counterfeit. It's only a temporary fix with a false appeal. A substitute can be likened unto to a zirconium diamond in that it is a cheap substitute for what is never going to be real. It has no real value.

Going through the substitute phase made me consider what many single people must go through every day. I never understood how single men and women could get entangled with someone with limited vision, no positive dreams, no goals, nor future plans for themselves. I personally experienced being entangled with a person who had a limited supply of everything I wanted and needed to release my past. I needed someone who was a true Christian whom I could trust with all my heart. I needed a mature, loving, caring, nurturing gentleman who would not be a short-term fix for the relationship I desired. I was trying to get something from someone who was unable to give what they did not have.

A short-term relationship with a person who is unable to give what they do not have will block you from God's perfect will for your life. I allowed the temporary man to abuse me by drawing me into listening to his false promises. In my desperation to fill a void, I accepted his degrading ways. I believed him when he said he would change and stop abusing me. But God, in His matchless love and mercy stopped me. Before I became completely entangled, I came to understand that the only person I could change was myself. Consequently, I started to look inside myself and reflect on why I would allow someone to abuse me. One reason may have been that in my younger years I repeatedly heard the phrase "half of a man is better than none at all." Believing in this false and old bondage saying of many years past hindered me from releasing myself from this substitute relationship.

We should never allow a person who is not whole to make us feel obligated to them. In fact, the Word of God tells us to love our neighbor as we love ourselves. Accepting abuse is not loving oneself. When we entangle ourselves by making wrong decisions and accepting the mistreatment of others, we choose to walk in disbelief and sin. Additionally, when we allow emotions to keep us in a temporary fix relationship, we become confused in our thinking. We cannot see a way out. The enemy tries to tell us that if we let go we will be alone. But he who is in Christ is never alone!

The cycle must be broken by receiving our fulfillment in God who has a wonderful plan for us here on earth. It is God's plan that we be fulfilled by walking in our God-ordained purpose. Do not try to use a limited person to soothe your pain and suffering. It is possible to release your pain, aloneness, and rejection by seeking help through God's people.

God has destiny helpers positioned to help you if you take the time to quiet your spirit and lay your fears and loneliness at the feet of Jesus. Release will come when the code of silence is broken. Release hurtful secrets that have kept you in an oppressive state of mind. The keys to releasing your mind so you can live again are in the Word of God. You have to pray-out, talk-out, cry-out, and work-out your troubles with God. He is the answer to every situation in your life, and He will give you the power to overcome and overtake!

But to you who fear My name the Sun of Righteousness shall arise with healing in His wings; and you shall go out and grow fat like stall-fed calves. Malachi 4:2 - (NKJV)

Chapter Twenty-One

THE ENEMY OF MY SOUL

I was a bubbly, joyous, playful, loving, and sweet child. In my grandma's loving home I didn't have a care in the world. I could often be heard squealing with joy as I ran around the yard playing with my brothers and sister. My tiny life was already a vibrant one, bursting with destiny and purpose. At seven years old, God was already grooming me. He had already filled me with love and laughter that a loveless and unhappy world would need. He had already blessed me with a smile that could light up the darkest corner. But the enemy also had a plan. His mission is to steal, kill, and destroy (John 10:10). If he could steal my joyous voice, kill my bubbly laughter, and destroy my innocence and sweetness, thousands of hurting people would stay chained in darkness for generations without hope and a deliverer.

The unthinkable things that happened to me in the 1940s and 50s were the first attacks from the pit of hell to steal my voice, and thus my purpose. Satan is the enemy of our souls, but his assignment is different for each of us based on our God-ordained destiny. For me, whom God would later call to travel the world to share His healing and delivering power to nations, the assignment was to take my voice. When the enemy saw that he was successful in that first attack to instill fear within me and close my mouth, he brought greater attacks in an attempt to shut me up for life. For over thirty years it looked like he was victorious. But then one day the Lord said, "That's enough!" He breathed His deep love into me and restored my voice. Things then began to move very quickly for me. God began to breathe new life and love into my marriage and family. Doors to ministry began to open to me all over the world. God brought destiny helpers and trained me at the feet of some of His best, and the rest has been history.

What have you allowed the enemy of your soul to steal from you? Think back to who you were before your painful experiences. What were you like? What were the dreams that bubbled in your heart? What life course did you have planned? As long as you are breathing, it is never too late to take your life back from the enemy of your soul. Even though I received my high school diploma as a teen mom by attending night school, I did not get to walk across the stage of achievement with my classmates. At 74 years old I took the walk across that stage. So pick yourself up from where the enemy has thrown you and receive your restoration from the throne of grace. *You are of God, little children, and have overcome them, because greater is He who is in you than he that is in the world! (1 John 4:4 NKJV)*

DECISION

Turning is not always easy, and believing in what cannot be seen, is even harder. That's where faith comes in. It's up to you to reprogram your mind to reach your destiny, despite your past. To fulfill the dreams that lay dormant within your heart, you must believe in yourself and have faith in God. When no one is looking, and it's just you and God, dare to dream again until your dreams become a reality.

Carmen believed that all things are possible through God, and that He would keep her foot from being snared again. She prayed to God to help her so that she could help others. She began to understand why God sent her through many trials and tribulations. She can now convey her message from personal experiences combined with new knowledge. God brought her into her trials, then through her tribulations. Now she is beyond the turning point and her dreams have become a reality.

Jesus said unto him, "If thou canst believe, all things are possible to him that believeth." Mark 9:23 – (NKJV).

Chapter Twenty-Two

THAT DOOR

Nothing hurts more than being disappointed by a person you thought would never hurt you who then makes you go through That Door.

Many wonder why I chose to call this book, *That Door*. Everything in life is a door. There are evil doors, painful doors, good doors, and destiny doors, etc. Life begins with a door. We enter the world through the womb, the door of our mothers. For nine months we are shielded, protected, and kept warm in a dark, but comfortable place. Suddenly we pass through the door and enter into a world full of light, color, and magnified sound.

When we take our first steps into a classroom as small children, we have entered the door of education, which leads to many more doors of endless possibilities. My life began happily in a peaceful, loving home. I had parents and grandparents who loved each other and loved God, so they therefore could love their children completely. I loved school and all the wonders and possibilities open to me there. But suddenly and without warning, my grandmother's front door became an evil door because of the filthy hand that touched and opened it.

My uncle opened the front door and then the door to his bedroom. I could not know as a child that those physical doors were opening up many unseen, wicked doors I would be forced to go through—the doors of pain, abuse, humiliation, degradation, sorrow, and trauma. These doors led me into pitch black rooms where fear, insecurity, and low self-esteem were developed. The darkness was like a thick, powerful hand that choked my voice. The demonic hand led me to even darker doors—doors of abuse in different forms, accusation, self-condemnation, self-pity, and self-hatred. Finally, I was led to the darkest door of all, the door of desired suicide.

It was at that place that the voice of God thunderously said, "Enough!" In His love and mercy, His mighty hand reached down and broke the fingers off the hand holding my voice. His strong arm pulled me out of the darkness and led me to new, bright, and colorful doors. The first big and inviting door was the door of forgiveness. This time I trusted the hand that led me. As I crossed the threshold, other magnificent doors appeared—doors of healing, love, joy, peace, and freedom. These doors led me to the inner sanctum of ministry. Behind those doors were thousands of broken, weeping people looking for the same deliverance I found.

If you have been forced to walk through evil doors, ask God to shine His light on the door of freedom and then walk *through it* and out! Many stay locked in dark rooms because they do not look up to the Light of heaven and ask Him to shine down on the escape route.

Some want to scream out for someone to hear them, but a python spirit squeezes and chokes their voice. When he thinks he has destroyed them completely, he puts his tail in their nose to see if they are still breathing. But in that place where it looks and feels like it is over, God will reach down and strangle the python.

It is in the darkest place that God will send destiny helpers with loving hands to pull you out and into God's glorious plan for your life. Ask God to make you sensitive to recognize your destiny helpers. Take God's strong and loving hand and walk through the doors of faith, hope, love, and believing what the Word of God says about you. Get up and walk through *That Door* to total healing, victory, and purpose! Your glorious journey is *just beginning!*

IMAGE

God had created Carmen in His image. Carmen was perfectly formed and very intelligent. God had a plan for her to go through the doors of identity crises, then grow into a stronger adult to help others who suffered some of the same pains. Our loving God has a plan for all of us, but we must listen and follow His instructions in the Word of God. His instructions are the blueprint for every success. If we choose to attain anything apart from God, we choose the door of separation and we will eventually perish from lack of a relationship with Him. The relationship we cultivate with Him through His Word will reveal who we are and why we were created.

Sometimes we can get so wrapped up in what we think we need that we forget who we are. We become altogether different, reaching for straws, and trying to make things happen the way we want them to. Instead, we should be looking unto the One who created us, the One who knows us better than we know ourselves because we were created in His image.

We must all take a deeper look at ourselves to make sure we are not causing the stress in our own lives. After taking that look, we must evaluate, re-evaluate, and prioritize what we are doing to make the necessary changes required to move to the next level in life.

When you seek help from your pastors and mentors, and pray to God, positive changes will come about in your life. You must persevere and be steadfast in your belief that God will help you. He is waiting for you and is holding open countless, magnificent doors of victory for you. Step in and take all He has for you!

Yet in all these things we are more that conquerors through Him who loved us. For I am persuaded that neither death nor life, nor angels nor principalities nor powers, nor things present nor things to come, nor height nor depth, nor any other created thing, shall be able to separate us from the love of God which is in Christ Jesus our Lord. Romans 8:37-39 – (NKJV)

The Epitaph

"A CIVILIZED SOCIETY"

My old mindset and self-image have forever changed from needing validation and the acceptance of man to accepting the wonder that I am in Christ Jesus. In Webster's New World Dictionary, Third College Edition, the meaning of an epitaph is an inscription on a tomb or gravestone in memory of the person buried there.

Self-discovery through the Word of God must be in place to receive a real release of the mind, so that one can truly live and forgive. My mindset had to die for me to be whom God created me to be. Jesus died to release us from the bondage of sin, for us to live abundant lives. For me to release my mind from past hurts, pain, and disappointments, I prayed for direction from God and sought out the counsel of my mentors. I asked God to show me the truth of His Word through spending quality time with Him. I needed to see the Word of God in a different light from what I learned as a child. Through getting to know God's Word, I found myself. I received the release that I needed to forgive others as well as myself. My old mindset was that of the prodigal son when he was in the hog pen. The hog pen is a most unfit place for human beings. My life was like that smelly hog pen because of the bad choices and decisions I did not think through as a young adult. Both sides of my family had set the tone for my life in making bad choices and decisions when I was just a child. In my later years, God gave me a Christian mentor who prayed with me regularly.

We were able to discuss deep issues and come to resolutions that helped me to make responsible decisions toward building wholesome and healthy relationships. I am now able to deeply trust God's direction for my life with all my relationships. Therefore, I have decided to speak out about my traumatic experiences with a heart of unwavering forgiveness, compassion, and love. I have forgiven both sides of my family for their ignorance and fear of family exposure due to sexual abuse, manipulation, and control. Their ignorance was not out of a lack of love, but in a desire to protect us from what they felt would be harmful for us to know.

The secret code of sexual silence must be shattered by communication without fear of rejection to stop continued generational abuse. In this book and in my pamphlet, I talk about what we can and must do as a civilized society to break the silence and stop the detrimental cycle of abuse. In this civilized American society there is no excuse, no justification for an adult raping a child, nor for an adult forcefully violating another human being. Many people never recover from such travesties. Their destinies are never recovered because they stay silent and don't seek help. Although no one was killed, beaten, or physically maimed in my maternal family, the sexual abuse existed in my maternal bloodline. I was a closet victim. The word 'special' in my family had a meaning all its own. I did not understand what the word truly meant until I was an adult. It has taken many decades for me to process the traumatic experiences and receive God's help as an adult. My educational and

Christian mentors, as well as instructional courses at an accredited college, have promoted and fostered my recovery and healing toward becoming a complete and useful vessel in the Master's hands.

Now that you have read this book, my prayer is that it will cause you to look at what you are allowing to hold you back from becoming complete. Your story might not be my story, but you do have one. This epitaph is a short composition written as a tribute to the past that contributed to the writing of this book. Because of my history with God, I knew He would not fail me.

As you begin to trust in God, you will begin to see your troubles shift into God's hand. Once the shifting begins, you will be able to forgive and bury your past that tried to keep you from fulfilling your destiny on earth. To seek help, you must reach out to a church and/or a Christian organization. Many Christian organizations offer the support and services that will help you to break the code of silence. Speaking about the abuse you have suffered will help you to release your pain and rejection to fulfill your God-ordained purpose on earth. Be forever mindful that a temporary short-term relationship will hinder you from your destiny and negative moral adjustments will be made to your very character through deceit and lies. It is the enemy who preys on singles, widows, and those who are going through periods of grief. He doesn't want you to use your God-given gifts and talents for the kingdom of God. But God, Your Creator and Redeemer, has the final say. He will get the glory in your life when you remember who you are and what He has done for you. If you should find someone whom you think you're getting emotionally involved with, take him to your pastor. Your pastor is your safety zone. Do not negate the shepherd whom God has placed in your life when making any life-altering decisions.

DEFINITIONS

MOLESTATION: Sexual assault or abuse of a person, especially a woman or child. The action of pestering or harassing someone in an aggressive or persistent manner.

INCEST: Sexual relations between people classed as being too closely related to marry each other. The crime of having sexual intercourse with a parent, child, sibling, or grandchild.

RAPE: Unlawful sexual activity and usually sexual intercourse carried out forcibly or under threat of injury against a person's will or with a person who is beneath a certain age or incapable of valid consent because of mental illness, mental deficiency, intoxication, unconsciousness, or deception. An act or instance of robbing or despoiling or carrying away a person by force. An outrageous crime of violation.

FROM THE HEART OF DR. IRENE HUSTON

Your life was not just created for you. God created each one of us with the ability to touch the life of someone who is also going through something we have already experienced. You were created for a time such as this. What is holding you back? It is up to you to take the lid off your potential. Do not block your own progress. Many people have turmoil in their life, but it does not have to end in despair. Victory is yours for the taking if you just believe and let the Word of God be activated in your life. Your God-ordained purpose will include the drama that is yet to unfold on the pages of your life still to be written.

Almost every vision and goal I ever had has come to pass in some phase of my life. I attended a modeling school as a young teen. In my later years I established a high-fashion clothing store, did interior design of homes, became a pastor, and received three college degrees. The one dream that did not manifest in the natural realm was my desire to become a pediatric nurse, but God's sovereignty revealed a deeper plan. He would use me to deliver thousands of women from wounds not reachable with a nurse's hand. The pastorship was not in my vision at all, but it was God's desired road for me to take His healing and deliverance around the world.

Take a good long look at yourself in the mirror and then forget what you see because you will not remain that image. You are daily evolving into the beautifully transformed woman that God, in His mercy and love, intended for you to be from the beginning of time.

Know that no matter what happens in life, your dreams will breathe when you put them into motion through forgiveness and release. Never give up on the dreams God has placed in your heart. You were created to do great things for God, things only *you* can do in this life. There are no carbon copies of you. Your fingerprints are unique, and every one of the hairs on your head are numbered. You are an original masterpiece designed to take hold of your purpose. Don't settle for less than God's best because you were created to fulfill the glorious plan which God has in store for you.

ABOUT THE AUTHOR

Dr. Irene Huston was born to serve God by serving people in every area. She was born on May 24, 1938, in Collins, Mississippi. She is the daughter of Leroy and Dovie Huston. She is one of five children. Dr. Huston was just a little girl during a fascinating time in the context of 20th century history. Her family was part of the "Second Great Migration", where more than five million African Americans from the South moved to the North, Midwest, and West to escape the torment of racism and unfair labor practices. Her family's journey began in the 1940's as her father sought a better life for his family and moved to Berkeley, California.

Dr. Huston received and committed her life to Christ at the age of 16. Her testimony is that of family restoration and "standing in the gap" for families. She has been a trailblazer and pioneer for the Kingdom of God for fifty years. She received her first ordination to preach the Gospel in 1970 from Pastor Alfred A. Watson of Ollie Grove Pentecostal Baptist Church in Berkeley, California. She was ordained to International Ministry by the late Archbishop Benson Idahosa of Nigeria, West Africa. Her evangelistic travels have taken her throughout the United States and to many foreign countries. She has ministered the gospel to thousands around the world, including Bangalore and Madras, India; Benin City, Nigeria; London, England; Jerusalem, Israel; St. Martin; and Petit Valle; Trinidad. Dr. Huston's life and ministry were greatly impacted by some world-changing women of God. She received impartation in ministering the Word through her travels and mentorship under Dr. Ernestine C. Reems. She attributes her confidence and uncompromising stability in the call of God to Dr. Beverly "BAM" Crawford's spiritual guidance, and Dr. Ernestine Sanders who encouraged her to attend theological seminary.

Dr. Irene received her Bachelor of Arts degree in Theology from International Seminary in Plymouth, Florida; a Master of Arts in Education from Antioch Christian University in Denver, Colorado; and her Doctor of Divinity degree from Southeast Clergy University, St. Louis, Missouri. She also received a Bachelor degree in Psychology from Phoenix University.

In 1985 she founded Global Christian Ministries in Richmond, California, which she still pastors today. She received the ordination of Apostle from The World Outreach Association and is currently Senior Overseer to three ministries in addition to her Bay Area headquarters. She is also founder of Irene's Women of Faith Foundation, Global Christian Academy (Grades K-12), and Global Seminary.

In 1992 Dr. Irene received a contract with the Oakland Warriors Basketball Franchise to design uniforms for their dancers and band members. Her love for fashion materialized in 1998 as realized a personal entrepreneurial goal and opened a boutique, Irene's Apparel, in El Sobrante, California. In 2000, she met her second goal by opening a hair salon, GCM & Company, of which she was co-owner.

Dr. Irene has been invited to participate in a wide spectrum of programs including conferences, seminars, panel forums, and community events. She has been a co-host on the 700 Club, a panelist for the Bay Area Black Media Coalition concerning "Religion on The Airwaves," a lecturer at San Jose State University, and was a panelist for the Coalition of Black Trade Unionists. She also taught a class at the Adult School in the Richmond Unified School District. Dr. Huston is known for one of the first All Women Evangelistic Conference, non-affiliated in Oakland, California. The late Ruth Carter Stapleton, sister of President Jimmy Carter, was a keynote speaker. Women from cities across California and the nation were in attendance. Dr. Huston was also invited to sit next to President Jimmy Carter when he visited San Francisco, California in 1976. She was also invited by the Honorable Jack Kingston to attend the Third Annual First Lady Luncheon given by First Lady Laura Bush in Washington D.C, all expenses paid. She was also invited to the White House Ball. Dr. Huston has also received numerous invitations from The City of Richmond's Recreation and Cultural Services Division and the Martin Luther King Commemorative Program Committee as guest speaker for their programs. She is President & CEO of Global Reaching Out, Inc., a non-profit community-based organization which provides counseling services, food, and clothing for the less fortunate. Dr. Irene was awarded a *Certificate for the Betterment of Richmond* and has received many Proclamations by the Mayor of Richmond. She also received the *Contra Costa County Dr. Martin Luther King Jr. 2000 Honorable Mention Humanitarian of the Year*

Award and was Mistress of Ceremony for the MLK Awards in 2001. In 2003, she was the recipient of the *Pastor of the Year* award from the C.O.G.I.C. Women's Department and was inducted into the national *Who's Who of American Executives* for four years. For her 75th birthday she was congratulated as pastor, founder, inspirational faith leader, teacher, and humanitarian by congresswoman Barbara Lee of the 13th district. She was recognized for her selfless motivation to create space for people to hear the Word of God and feel closer to Him, and for her powerful message of prayer and Spirit-filled leadership. For her 80th birthday, she was honored by the 116th Congress of the House of Representatives for her lifetime achievements and valuable contributions to Contra Costa County and the larger Bay Area. The honor read in part, "Congressional Record: Proceedings and Debates of the 116th Congress, First Session—House of Representatives on the birthday of Dr. Irene Huston—Extension of Remarks by Hon. Mark Desaulner of California in the House of Representatives—Madame Speaker, I rise today to recognize the service of a long-time community leader, Dr. Irene Huston..."

Apostle Irene has published *Opportunities Through Crisis*, a motivational book on how to handle life's crisis by precept and example (which is now in its fifth printing.) She has also published several spiritually enlightening booklets including *THAT, How to Pray for your Lost Loved Ones,* and *"Irene's Motivational Thoughts & Inspirations."* She has hosted several weekly television programs including *God's Finest Hour* and *Best Day Ever* which aired on KTLN

Channel 68. The broadcasts also had multiple California Contra Costa County and northern California airings on Comcast Cable channel 42 and other channels. Nationally, her programs were aired on the Word network.

Apostle Irene is the widow of Elder Ralph Huston, her husband of fifty years. She is the loving mother of six children, fourteen grandchildren, and sixteen great-grandchildren. Her husband, children, mother, sons-in-law, and sister all worked together in ministry. Apostle Irene walks in the five-fold apostolic anointing. Because of the strong prophetic teaching anointing God has graciously given her, Dr. Huston has become a *"disturbing element"* in the body of Christ which has transitioned her to the platinum level in ministry. As she preaches the Word of God with power and authority, the Holy Spirit engulfs the atmosphere with healing, deliverance, and restoration, destroying every yoke of the enemy. She has mentored many sons and daughters in ministry who are now pastoring churches and doing other note-worthy works for the Lord in their respective communities.

Dr. Huston has found that life is truly not over. According to Haggai 2:9, *"The glory of this latter house shall be greater than of the former,"* saith the Lord of hosts; *"and in this place will I give peace,"* saith the Lord of hosts. Her latter is truly greater than her former as she envisions new heights for Global Christian Ministries in Richmond, California; and new Spirit-filled and highly regarded women's conferences to be hosted in the Bay Area. She is still in high demand. Dr. Huston is now mentoring a new generation of young ladies and women in ministry. She has now added playwright to her list of accomplishments as she is now directing the play *THAT DOOR* which will be released soon. Dr. Huston often says, "I don't think I had the chance to be a kid."

Doctorate, Theology   Bachelor, Psychology

"And we know that all things work together for good to them that love God, to them who are the called according to His purpose." Romans 8:28

ENCOURAGEMENT FROM THE AUTHOR

For those of you who may not have gone through what I had to endure from the age of seven, but have fought your own individual and relevant battles, the purpose of this book is to encourage you to hold fast to your dreams. Never allow anything to make you lose them. If you allow yourself to forget and do not dwell in a place of unforgiveness, then God will cause every dream you dream to come to pass. I wrote this book to encourage those of you who are not moving forward in your dreams or visions because of some doorstop that got in your way. You may have given up, but I want to say to you--take care and move forward. Your life is precious. 3 John 1:2 says, "Beloved, I wish above all things that thou mayest prosper and be in health, even as thy soul prospereth." God wants you to have your every dream if you allow Him to be first in your life. The bad things that happened to me hindered me; but I never allowed myself to stop dreaming, and that's why I am where I am today. My desire is that you see that God will bring you up and out, but you have to stay the course. Do not let distractions take you off track. When negative circumstances happen, all you need is a bounce! Thank you for purchasing this book. Let it be a solution to your life. I love you! Apostle/Dr. Irene Huston

"Lioness of Power"

To book Dr. Apostle Irene Huston for a speaking engagement, book signing, or special event, contact: drirenehuston@gmail.com

****

To purchase additional copies of this book, or to purchase other titles by Dr. Irene MOMMA Huston, including *"Opportunities Through Crisis,"* contact drirenehuston@gmail.com

****

RESOURCES:
YWCA Silicon Valley 24-hour Rape Crisis Hotline (408) 287-3000 or (650) 493-7273

Global Christian Ministries
P.O. BOX 808 Pinole, CA 94564

****

Thank you for your purchase! We hope you enjoyed the book. Don't forget to submit your review at Amazon.com. We appreciate your support!

Made in the USA
Middletown, DE
15 June 2024

55585612R00119